HIDDEN HISTORY
of CIVIL WAR
OREGON

HIDDEN HISTORY
of CIVIL WAR
OREGON

RANDOL B. FLETCHER

THE
History
PRESS

Published by The History Press
Charleston, SC 29403
www.historypress.net

Back cover: Statue at Portland GAR Cemetery. *Photo by Merry Crimi*; Battle flag of the 38th Virginia. *Courtesy of the Museum of the Confederacy, Richmond, Virginia. Photo by Katherine Wetzel*; Portland and Mount Hood, circa 1903. *Courtesy of Oregon Historical Society #bb000227.*

First published 2011
Second printing 2013

Manufactured in the United States

ISBN 978.1.60949.424.7

Library of Congress Cataloging-in-Publication Data
Fletcher, Randol B.
Hidden history of Civil War Oregon / Randol B. Fletcher.
p. cm.
Includes bibliographical references.
ISBN 978-1-60949-424-7
1. Oregon--History--Civil War, 1861-1865. 2. Oregon--History--Civil War,
1861-1865--Biography. 3. Oregon--History, Local. 4. Oregon--Biography. 5. Portland
(Or.)--Biography. 6. United States--History--Civil War, 1861-1865--Campaigns. 7. United
States--History--Civil War, 1861-1865--Biography. I. Title.
E526.F55 2011
979.5'041--dc23
2011032573

This book is dedicated to my great-great-grandfathers
who served in the War Between the States:

Private John Hays, 25th Indiana Infantry, USA

Private Jeptha Pond, 21st Tennessee Cavalry, CSA

Sergeant Jonathan Pringle, Ballard's Company, Arkansas Infantry, CSA

Private Harvey Henderson Shelton, 6th Illinois Cavalry, USA

As we commemorate the 150th anniversary of the American Civil War, it is paramount that we remember the sacrifices of that generation, North and South. There are no longer any Civil War veterans to tell what they did in that war; we must tell their story for them.

Contents

CONTENTS

Guarding the Homefront

Oregon Civil War Regiments

Hurrah for Jeff Davis and damn the man that won't! Phillip Mulkey paraded up and down the streets of Eugene City shouting the praises of Confederate president Jefferson Davis. Crowds of Union supporters surrounded Mulkey, yelling back at him, and the scene quickly devolved into chaos bordering on violence. Word was sent to summon the provost guard, and troops from the 1st Oregon Volunteer Infantry double-timed downtown and placed Mulkey under arrest. As the soldiers were leading Mulkey away, someone handed the unrepentant Rebel a glass of water, and Mulkey defiantly raised the glass and drank a toast to Davis. Thus began the so-called Long Tom Rebellion, a little-known chapter in the hidden history of Civil War Oregon.

At the outbreak of the Civil War, the whole of the Federal army numbered barely ten thousand men. Most of the soldiers were stationed at remote forts in the West, and Oregon had a fair amount of those troops. The 4th U.S. Infantry was based at Fort Vancouver and had small posts throughout Oregon and Washington Territories. Ulysses S. Grant was stationed in Oregon Territory briefly in 1852. Future Union general Philip Sheridan had a much longer tenure serving as a junior officer in Oregon from 1855 to 1861. Years after the Civil War, both Grant and Sheridan made triumphant tours of Oregon. The cities of Grants Pass and Sheridan are named in their honor.

When the Confederates fired on Fort Sumter, President Lincoln called for volunteers, and each state was given a quota of troops it was expected to provide. Tiny Oregon proved to be problematic for the Lincoln administration. Although Oregon was a free state and had voted for Lincoln in the election,

Before achieving fame as a Civil War general, Phil Sheridan served six years as a junior officer in Oregon. *Library of Congress.*

its governor was a proslavery Democrat known as Honest John Whiteaker, and he was not keen on sending Oregon boys three thousand miles away to fight against his political kin. Lincoln pulled the regulars from Oregon and sent them to the front, which left the state's small white population living in fear of reprisals from the suppressed native people.

HORSE SOLDIERS

The army replaced the regulars with volunteer soldiers from California. Then, as now, Oregonians resented California influence. After gaining assurances that local troops would remain in the Northwest, Governor Whiteaker commissioned state senator Thomas Cornelius a colonel and ordered him to raise ten companies of cavalry. Cornelius, a veteran of the Cayuse War, was a Republican from Missouri, so he appealed to both the northern and southern factions within the state. After the war, Cornelius became president of the Oregon Senate and later built Cornelius Pass Road. He ran unsuccessfully for governor in 1886. The town of Cornelius, Oregon, is named in his honor, and he is buried in the Methodist Church Cemetery there.

The Oregon cavalry was assigned to escort immigrants on the Oregon Trail and protect miners in eastern Oregon. They fought a number of skirmishes with bands of indigenous people but suffered just ten battle deaths, including one Native American scout from the Warm Springs tribe. The men of the Oregon cavalry were well paid for their time. While privates in the army drew $13 per month, Oregon cavalry troopers received an additional $100 bounty and 160 acres of land at the end of three years' service. Despite above-average pay, Oregon soldiers were susceptible to gold fever. A gold strike in eastern Oregon in 1862 led to ten thousand mining claims being filed that year. Desertion became a major problem as soldiers sent to guard the miners snuck out of camp to try their luck in the gold fields. Nearly 150 men of the Oregon regiments were charged with desertion.

When the fortune-hunting deserters were caught, punishment varied from having their heads shaved to six months of hard labor chained to twelve-pound balls. A few repeat offenders received the ultimate sentence for wartime desertion: death by firing squad. In all but one case, the executions were stayed and the condemned men were pardoned.

The unlucky soldier was a twenty-four-year-old Irishman who had enlisted in the 1st Oregon Cavalry in Jacksonville. Private Francis Ely not only deserted his regiment, but he also took his government-issued mount with him. He was caught on the road to the gold fields and taken to Fort Walla Walla to face court-martial. Convicted of desertion and as a horse thief, he was sentenced to death. On the day set for Ely's execution, his captain was so certain that a reprieve would be issued that he posted sentries along the road every twelve miles so that any arriving courier could be rushed to the fort. No message of mercy arrived, and at two o'clock in the afternoon of March 6, 1864, Ely was seated on his coffin in the back of a wagon and driven to the place of execution. The Irishman was stood against a high wooden fence, and a black hood was drawn over his head. A firing squad blasted a volley of four musket balls into his chest. One year later, President Lincoln granted amnesty to all army deserters. Ely is buried in an unmarked grave in the Fort Walla Walla Military Cemetery. He was the only soldier on the Pacific coast put to death by the military in the Civil War.

WEBFOOT VOLUNTEERS

In 1863, Portland's Addison Gibbs was sworn in as Oregon's first Republican governor. With Republicans in the top offices, Oregon's southern Democrats were driven underground. The state swirled with intrigue as rumors spread of secessionists caching arms and of a shadowy organization known as the Knights of the Golden Circle planning to form an independent republic on the Pacific coast. Joseph Lane, who became governor of Oregon Territory only after Abraham Lincoln turned down the job, was unfairly implicated in the plots. With the cavalry away patrolling the high desert and guarding the coast reservations, the main cities in Oregon had almost no formal military presence and relied on militia for protection. In response to the perceived threat, Governor Gibbs obtained permission to raise a second regiment of Oregonians.

The 1st Oregon Volunteer Infantry was formed in November 1864. At full strength, the regiment consisted of ten one-hundred-man companies. Captain George B. Currey of the Oregon cavalry was promoted to colonel and appointed commanding officer of the infantry. Currey was a prominent Oregon pioneer, lawyer and newspaperman. After the war, Currey held a number of Federal positions in Oregon before retiring to LaGrande, where he died in 1906. He is buried in the IOOF Cemetery in LaGrande.

Currey's infantry was uniformed in regulation long, dark blue frock coats, sky blue trousers and wool kepis with a leather bill. They were armed with .58-caliber muskets. Oregon infantry recruits were paid a $150 upfront enlistment bonus. Currey sent his men on extensive patrols and scouting operations, but unlike the swift horse cavalry, infantry moved slowly, and for the most part, the mounted Indians they were chasing simply rode away when the foot soldiers approached. Despite all the rumors of secret Confederate cliques in Oregon, most Rebel activity was limited to raising a Confederate flag here and there, and those flags were quickly torn down by loyal citizens. Life in the webfoot army was best described as monotony broken only by tedium and complaining about the food. When a company of Oregon infantry arrived at Fort Hoskins in 1864, they found barrels of flour and salt pork dated 1852. The only fatalities suffered by the 1st Oregon Infantry came from disease or accident. Their most prominent operation came in the aforementioned Long Tom Rebellion.

INSURRECTION IN EUGENE CITY

It was May 6, 1865, when Philip Mulkey took to the streets of Eugene City hollering hurrahs for Jefferson Davis. The country was still mourning President Lincoln, who had been assassinated just three weeks earlier. Davis, his armies defeated, was fleeing for his life in fear of being hanged for treason. Mulkey, a pioneer Gospel preacher, had crossed the plains by covered wagon, arriving in Oregon from Missouri in 1853. He took a donation land claim west of Eugene, and by all accounts he was a respected and law-abiding citizen until his public outburst and arrest at the end of the Civil War.

As Reverend Mulkey sat in the Lane County jail, a pro-Union lynch mob decided to take matters into its own hands. In response to the threat of frontier justice, pro-Confederate sympathizers from Mulkey's home area along the Long Tom River were arming themselves to come to their neighbor's rescue. Guards were shoved aside as the Union rioters busted down the jail door. Mulkey pulled a hidden knife from his coat and slashed the first man through the door. The sight of the bloody blade caused the mob to pause just long enough for the Oregon infantry to arrive at the double-quick. The army surrounded the jail and dispersed the crowd. Late that night, the soldiers slipped Mulkey down to the river and put him under guard on a steamboat, and he was taken to the stockade at Fort Vancouver. With Mulkey out of town, the Long Tom men had no one to liberate, so they went home. Four days after Mulkey's arrest, fugitive Jefferson Davis was captured in Georgia, and the Confederate States of America was extinguished.

Mulkey spent three months in prison, and when paroled, he filed suit against the government for false arrest and violation of his free speech rights. He sought $10,000 in compensation. After two years and fourteen court hearings, Mulkey settled for $200. The war over, Mulkey returned to his calling as a circuit-riding minister. It is said that he performed over one hundred weddings in Lane County. Reverend Mulkey was ninety-one when he passed away in 1893. He is buried in Mulkey Cemetery in Eugene.

OREGON VETERANS

Once the Civil War was over, the regular army returned to the Pacific Northwest. The Oregon cavalry mustered out in November 1866, and the infantry followed it out of service in July 1867. Several of the Oregon veterans went on to distinguished postwar careers. Notable among them are:

REUBEN F. MAURY was one of the few professional soldiers in the Oregon volunteer regiments. He graduated from West Point in 1846 in a class that included George Pickett and Stonewall Jackson. After serving in the Mexican War, Maury was an Oregon pioneer of 1852. Settling in Jackson County, he volunteered for service during the Civil War and was appointed major of the 1st Oregon Cavalry before eventually being promoted and named as the army's last commander of the District of Oregon. Colonel Maury is buried in Jacksonville Cemetery.

JOHN MARSHALL MCCALL was an Oregon pioneer of 1851 and served as a captain in the Oregon cavalry. After the war, McCall founded Ashland Woolen Mills and the Bank of Ashland. He was the first treasurer of the City of Ashland and later served as mayor. In 1876, he was elected to the state legislature on the People's ticket. In 1883, Governor Zenas Moody appointed McCall brigadier general of the Oregon militia. General McCall is buried in Ashland Cemetery.

WILLIAM HILLEARY is the author of the important Oregon history *A Webfoot Volunteer: The Diary of William M. Hilleary, 1864–1866.* The diary recounts Hilleary's service as a corporal in Company F of the 1st Oregon Infantry. After the war, Hilleary became a schoolteacher and was active in the Grange movement, becoming a strong advocate for rural free mail delivery, a postal savings banking system and a canal across Nicaragua. In 1896, he was elected master of the Oregon State Grange and became a member of the Board of Regents of Oregon Agricultural College. A member of Brownsville GAR Post 49, he was the son of James Hilleary and Nancy Morris and was a direct descendant of Peregrine White, the first child born on the *Mayflower*. He married Liebe Cornelius. Their farm south of Turner was called Red Oak. Hilleary is buried in Twin Oaks Cemetery in Turner.

ROYAL BENSELL joined the 4th California Infantry when it arrived in the Willamette Valley. As an Oregonian in a California regiment, he served three years in the army and after the war wrote the book *All Quiet on the Yamhill* about his experiences. It is Hilleary's and Bensell's accounts that provide the best description of the dreariness of soldiering the frontier. Bensell was one of the first white men to settle on Yaquina Bay and served four terms as mayor of Newport. He is buried in Eureka Cemetery in Newport.

WILLIAM C. CUSICK was eleven years old when he walked the Oregon Trail from Illinois to the Willamette Valley with an 1853 wagon train. He was teaching school when he volunteered for duty with the Oregon infantry and served as a sergeant in Company F. While serving along the Nez Perce reservation, Cusick developed an interest in wild plants. After the war, he settled in the Powder River Valley of eastern Oregon, where he became a pioneering wildlife botanist. Cusick began collecting native plant samples from all over the state. Oregon State University has about 4,500 Cusick specimens in its herbarium, and the University of Oregon purchased his ten-thousand-page catalogue of flora. Cusick died at his brother's home in Union and is buried in the Pioneer Cemetery there. He was buried as a soldier and has a military headstone. At least twenty-seven species of native plants are named in Cusick's honor.

DAVID P. THOMPSON arrived in Portland driving sheep over the Oregon Trail. He became a wealthy railroad builder and served as a captain in the Oregon cavalry. While serving in the Oregon Senate, Thompson was appointed governor of Idaho Territory by President Grant. He later served two terms as mayor of Portland and was named U.S. minister to Turkey by President Benjamin Harrison. Thompson was the 1890 Republican candidate for Oregon governor. He was a regent of the University of Oregon and president of the Oregon Humane Society. The elk statue fountain in downtown Portland was a gift to the city from Thompson. He is buried in River View Cemetery in Portland.

Portland mayor and Civil War veteran David Thompson donated this fountain, shown here in 1901, which is located in the middle of Southwest Main Street between Third and Fourth Avenues. The water basin was designed as a drinking trough for horses and dogs. *Courtesy of City of Portland Archives A2004-002.6703.*

Colonel Thomas Monteith, one of the founders of Albany. *Courtesy of Monteith Historical Society.*

JOHN T. APPERSON of Oregon City was the steamboat captain who piloted Senator Edward D. Baker from Salem to Portland on his way to Washington. Inspired by Baker, Apperson joined the Oregon cavalry and hoped to serve under Baker, a dream that ended when Baker was killed at Ball's Bluff. After the war, Apperson served in the Oregon House and Senate and was elected sheriff of Clackamas County. He is buried in Mountain View Cemetery in Oregon City.

DANIEL W. APPLEGATE was the son of famous Oregon pioneer Jesse Applegate. The Applegates were one of the most influential families in the early days of Oregon and were pro-Union and pro-Lincoln. Daniel, a second lieutenant, was one of five Applegate men to serve in the 1st Oregon Volunteer Infantry. Following his military service, Daniel Applegate engaged in a number of business ventures in Douglas County, including farming, mining and working for the railroad. He is buried in Applegate Cemetery in Yoncalla.

LOUIS T. BARIN served as a first sergeant in the Oregon cavalry. After the war, he became a lawyer, served in the Oregon legislature and was elected mayor of Oregon City. President Harrison appointed Barin U.S. marshal. He, too, is buried in Mountain View Cemetery.

THOMAS MONTEITH, along with his older brother Walter, founded the city of Albany. In 1863 and 1864, Thomas served as a colonel in the Oregon volunteer militia. Unlike the full-time soldiers of the Oregon infantry and cavalry, the Oregon militia was what some called a "drill and chowder society." They would meet regularly for drill and then spend time socializing. Militia members were paid two dollars for each day of duty, and able-bodied men who chose not to serve in the militia were taxed two dollars annually. Monteith's sword is currently on display at the Monteith House Museum. Colonel Monteith is buried in Albany's Riverside Cemetery.

THOMAS J. LEE, in contrast to the bearded frontiersmen of the Oregon regiments, didn't need to shave. He was just fifteen when he enlisted in the Oregon infantry, and he served for two years. Although the official age for joining the army was eighteen, at least 107 under-age enlistees served the Beaver State. After the war, Lee returned to school, became a physician in Independence and represented Polk County in the Oregon legislature. Dr. Lee is buried in Hilltop Cemetery in Independence.

OREGON SOLDIERS WHO DIED IN SERVICE DURING THE CIVIL WAR

NAME	REGIMENT	DATE OF DEATH	CAUSE OF DEATH
Pvt. James Alderson	Oregon Cavalry	5 Nov. 1866	Killed in action
Pvt. August Alexander	Oregon Infantry	10 Nov. 1864	Disease
Col. Edward D. Baker	California Brigade	21 Oct. 1861	KIA—Virginia

Name	Regiment	Date of Death	Cause of Death
Pvt. Edward G. Brown	Oregon Cavalry	6 Sep. 1863	Unknown
Sgt. Robert H. Casteel	Oregon Cavalry	7 April 1864	Missing presumed KIA
Pvt. George Chapin	Oregon Cavalry	16 July 1862	Disease
Sgt. Job C. Durphy	Oregon Cavalry	17 May 1864	Accident
Pvt. Francis Ely	Oregon Cavalry	3 March 1864	Executed for desertion
Pvt. Matthew Fitzsimmons	Oregon Cavalry	5 March 1865	Killed in action
Sgt. George Garber	Oregon Cavalry	17 Nov. 1865	Died of battle wounds
Pvt. Theodore Gould	Oregon Cavalry	26 Nov. 1863	Disease
Pvt. Stephen Halleck	Oregon Infantry	2 April 1866	Exposure
Cpl. James Harkinson	Oregon Cavalry	18 May 1864	Killed in action
Pvt. John Himbert	Oregon Cavalry	7 April 1864	Missing presumed KIA
Pvt. Cyrus R. Ingraham	Oregon Cavalry	7 April 1864	Missing presumed KIA
Pvt. James H. Irwin	Oregon Infantry	16 Nov. 1864	Drowned
Pvt. Bennett Kennedy	Oregon Cavalry	18 May 1864	Killed in action
Capt. James W. Lingenfelter	1st California Infantry	21 Sep. 1861	KIA—Virginia
Pvt. Charles Martin	Oregon Infantry	1 March 1865	Accident
Pvt. Perry B. McCord	Oregon Cavalry	9 April 1866	Unknown
Pvt. Isaac McKay	Oregon Infantry	5 Dec. 1865	Disease
Pvt. Amos Merrifield	Oregon Cavalry	5 April 1865	Drowned
Pvt. William Neece	Oregon Cavalry	22 Dec. 1862	Disease
Pvt. Thomas G. Reed	Oregon Cavalry	9 April 1862	Disease
Pvt. Thomas E. Shea	Oregon Cavalry	22 Dec. 1865	Unknown
Chief Stockelly	Warm Springs Scouts	6 June 1864	Died of battle wounds
Pvt. Samuel P. Strang	Oregon Cavalry	1864	Drunkenness
Pvt. Samuel Sutherland	Oregon Cavalry	26 Oct. 1864	Unknown
Pvt. Greenbury Tedrow	Oregon Cavalry	1 Feb. 1866	Disease
Pvt. Charles Thompson	Oregon Cavalry	3 Oct. 1863	Murdered
Lt. Stephen Watson	Oregon Cavalry	18 May 1864	Killed in action

The Hunt for John Wilkes Booth

Two Portland Men Who Chased Down the Assassin

The president has been shot! Trooper John Millington was standing guard duty west of Washington before dawn on April 15, 1865, when he was notified that President Lincoln had been shot at Ford's Theater the night before. The bugler sounded "Boots and Saddles," and Millington's regiment rode the outskirts of the city in an attempt to prevent the assassin from fleeing the capital. It was a gray Saturday, and a steady rainfall chilled the men of the 16th New York Cavalry as they joined thousands of other soldiers in an attempt to lock down the city. The mission was impossible, for the murderer and his accomplice had already made their way across the Potomac and slipped into Maryland. Later in the day, word was passed to the soldiers that the president had died and that well-known actor John Wilkes Booth had committed the dastardly deed.

The news of the president's death saddened and angered the soldiers. The boys in blue revered the president. They called him "Father Abraham," and it was the support of the military that had sealed Lincoln's reelection in 1864. For the first time in American history, troops in the field were allowed to vote, and they responded overwhelmingly, 70 percent or more, in favor of Abraham Lincoln.

A week before the assassination, Millington and his comrades in the 16th, including his pard Emory Parady, had celebrated joyously the news from Appomattox that Lee had surrendered to Grant. The war was won, and Millington and Parady had survived. Soon they would be going home to their native New York.

TROOPERS RECALLED FOR FUNERAL DUTY

After three days on patrol in an attempt to keep the assassination conspirators from leaving the city, the 16th New York Cavalry was recalled to Washington, where it was to take part in the president's funeral. Lincoln's body had been taken to the White House, where his funeral was held on Wednesday, April 19. After the service, twelve army sergeants carried the coffin and placed it in a horse-drawn carriage for the final trip down Pennsylvania Avenue to the Capitol. General Grant and President Andrew Johnson led the funeral procession, followed by a regiment of U.S. Colored Troops leading thousands of Union soldiers, including Parady, Millington and the rest of the 16th New York Cavalry. Behind the dignitaries and the regiments were forty thousand African Americans, the freeborn and the newly free, walking and holding one another's hands as they mourned. Hundreds of thousands of spectators lined the streets and filled every window, balcony and rooftop to witness the procession and pay their final respects. Witnesses to the event remarked on the size of the crowd and marveled at the absolute silence of the occasion, broken only by the muffled drums of the military escort. After lying in state at the Capitol, the president's body was loaded on a special train for his final trip to Springfield. Their solemn duty of the day complete, the soldiers of the 16th Cavalry returned to their barracks.

John Millington. *Courtesy of Steven G. Miller.*

Parady and Millington had served together for seven months, ever since Parady had joined the 16th in September 1864 and been assigned to Company H, where Millington served. Millington, at age twenty-one, was a seasoned veteran. Stocky and with dark, curly hair, Millington had been eighteen when the Civil War began, and he enlisted in the 93rd New York Infantry. The farm boy from Chester fought in several major engagements with the 93rd before contracting typhoid and receiving a disability discharge after the Battle of Fredericksburg. After spending a year at home recovering from the disease, Millington reenlisted in the cavalry.

Parady, age twenty, had grown up on his parents' farm near Beekmantown, about ninety miles from the Millington place. Emory's brother, Joe Parady, was already serving with the 16th New York when Emory enlisted. The Parady brothers and Millington had fought together against Confederate forces in numerous engagements and skirmishes throughout northern Virginia.

Five days after the funeral, Millington and Parady were chowing down in the barracks when they heard the first notes of "Boots and Saddles," the bugle call that orders cavalry to mount up. Normal military protocol was ignored for the sake of speed. Lieutenant Edward Doherty, the officer in charge of the detail, took command of the first twenty-five men to hit the saddle. Doherty added a sergeant from his own troop and led his men to the corner of Fourteenth Street and Pennsylvania Avenue, across from the Willard Hotel. There, two men in civilian clothes—agents from the National Detective Police, precursor of the Secret Service—met the troopers. The detectives led the cavalry to the Washington Navy Yard, where the men and their horses were loaded onboard a steamship, which headed down the Potomac.

On board the ship, Doherty showed his men a set of three photographs. The troopers did not recognize two of the men, but the third portrait was clearly that of the famous actor John Wilkes Booth. The soldiers' hearts leapt with excitement; they were going after the assassins! The largest manhunt in history was underway. Doherty's detachment was told that Booth had crossed the Potomac near Port Tobacco, and they were instructed to seize any man resembling the pictures.

At about ten o'clock that night, the troopers landed on shore and began a hard target search of every residence, warehouse, farmhouse, henhouse, outhouse and doghouse in the area. Talking in whispers, the cavalry traveled light. Armed only with pistols and sabers, Parady reported that they were ordered to secure the sabers to their saddles to reduce their clanking noise. In addition, the men carried no food or provisions, confiscating what they needed from local farms and houses, issuing Federal payment vouchers as compensation. The search party, one of hundreds of patrols scouring the countryside, caught a break in the manhunt early in the afternoon of the second day. While searching near Point Conway, Virginia, they questioned fisherman William Rollins. Asked if he had seen any strangers crossing the river in the last several days, Rollins reported that two men in a wagon—one man with a broken leg—had crossed the day before. Three Confederate soldiers on horseback accompanied the men in the wagon. Luther Baker, one of the detectives accompanying the cavalry, showed Rollins photographs of the three fugitives they sought. The first man pictured was John Surratt, and Rollins reported that he had not seen him. Rollins recognized the man in the second picture as being in the wagon with the man with the broken leg. That man was David Herold, who was seen outside Ford's Theater the night of the assassination. The third picture shown by the detective was identified as the man with the broken leg, John Wilkes Booth. They were on the right trail! Rollins had even more information to share. He reported that he recognized one of the Confederate soldiers as a local man named Willie Jett who had served with Mosby's Rangers. Rollins further volunteered that Jett was courting a local girl named Izora Goldman, whose father ran the Star Hotel near Bowling Green. Rollins was conscripted as a guide, and the cavalry mounted up and headed to find Jett.

The men of the 16th New York arrived in Bowling Green at midnight and quickly surrounded the hotel. They suspected Booth and his accomplices to be sleeping inside. Doherty and the second detective on the killer's trail, Everton Conger, pounded on the hotel door, and when the door was opened by Mrs. Goldman, they rushed past her with pistols in hand and ready for action. The Union soldiers hurried upstairs to find a man in his underclothes starting to rise from his bed. "Are you Jett?" they shouted, and when he answered in the affirmative, they seized the man and roughly hustled him down the stairs, dragging along the Goldmans' son Jesse. Under interrogation, Jett stated that he did not know who the two men in the wagon were except that they were Confederate soldiers who had gotten into some trouble in Maryland and needed a place to lay low. He stated he did not know where they had gone. After what Millington described as some "forcible persuasion," Jett asked to speak to Conger by himself.

Alone with the detective, Jett agreed to lead the search party to Booth and Herold's hideout on the condition that he did so under the appearance of force. Jett was concerned for his safety if he were to be seen as a Yankee collaborator, and he wanted no witnesses to his capitulation. Jett was permitted to dress as his horse was retrieved from the stable. The Confederate ranger then led the Federal men back up the road they had just traveled to the Garrett farm. Earlier that night, in their dash to the Star Hotel, the cavalry had thundered by Garrett's farm without stopping to search. They did not even notice that David Herold was standing plainly visible within the gates of the farm, watching the horsemen tear down the road. When Jett

SURRAT.   BOOTH.   HAROLD.

War Department, Washington, April 20, 1865,

$100,000 REWARD!

THE MURDERER

Of our late beloved President, Abraham Lincoln,

IS STILL AT LARGE.

$50,000 REWARD

Will be paid by this Department for his apprehension, in addition to any reward offered by Municipal Authorities or State Executives.

$25,000 REWARD

Will be paid for the apprehension of JOHN H. SURRATT, one of Booth's Accomplices.

$25,000 REWARD

Will be paid for the apprehension of David C. Harold, another of Booth's accomplices.

LIBERAL REWARDS will be paid for any information that shall conduce to the arrest of either of the above-named criminals, or their accomplices.

All persons harboring or secreting the said persons, or either of them, or aiding or assisting their concealment or escape, will be treated as accomplices in the murder of the President and the attempted assassination of the Secretary of State, and shall be subject to trial before a Military Commission and the punishment of DEATH.

Let the stain of innocent blood be removed from the land by the arrest and punishment of the murderers.

All good citizens are exhorted to aid public justice on this occasion. Every man should consider his own conscience charged with this solemn duty, and rest neither night nor day until it be accomplished.

EDWIN M. STANTON, Secretary of War.

DESCRIPTIONS.—BOOTH is Five Feet 7 or 8 inches high, slender build, high forehead, black hair, black eyes, and wears a heavy black moustache.

JOHN H. SURRAT is about 5 feet, 9 inches. Hair rather thin and dark; eyes rather light; no beard. Would weigh 145 or 150 pounds. Complexion rather pale and clear, with color in his cheeks. Wore light clothes of fine quality. Shoulders square; cheek bones rather prominent; chin narrow; ears projecting at the top; forehead rather low and square, but broad. Parts his hair on the right side; neck rather long. His lips are firmly set. A slim man.

DAVID C. HAROLD is five feet six inches high, hair dark, eyes dark, eyebrows rather heavy, full face, nose short, hand short and fleshy, feet small, instep high, round bodied, naturally quick and active, slightly closes his eyes when looking at a person.

NOTICE.—In addition to the above, State and other authorities have offered rewards amounting to almost one hundred thousand dollars, making an aggregate of about TWO HUNDRED THOUSAND DOLLARS.

Library of Congress.

indicated they were nearing the Garretts' place, Doherty slowed his column. Jett and Detective Baker opened the Garrett gate, and the 16th New York Cavalry charged at full gallop down the road to the farmhouse.

THE ASSASSINS ARE CORNERED

The barking of the dogs awakened Booth and Herold, who were asleep in the Garretts' tobacco barn. They soon heard the unmistakable sound of cavalry on fast approach. Farmer Richard Garrett, asleep in his house, also awoke and was on his front porch when the cavalry arrived in the blackness of night. Detectives Conger and Baker leapt from their saddles onto the porch and confronted the old man while half of the detachment, including Parady, was sent to search nearby barns. The detectives demanded to know the whereabouts of the two men who had visited that evening. Garrett replied that he knew nothing about any men being there, at which point Doherty ordered one of his men to fetch him a picket rope, saying, "We'll hang the old man and see if it will refresh his memory." Garrett had two sons, both recently returned from the war, who were hiding at the farm. At the mention of hanging, son John Garrett came out of the woods and said he would tell the detectives what they wanted to know. Before being given a chance to speak further, young Garrett was seized by Doherty, who pointed his revolver at Garrett's head. Conger demanded, "Where are they?" and the reply was, "The two men are in the barn." In that same instant, Parady heard voices coming from inside the tobacco barn, and he summoned his officer.

At the approach of cavalry, Booth and Herold attempted to flee, only to discover that the Garrett boys had locked them in the barn. The fugitives tried in vain to kick out the wood slats in order to escape, but the barn was solidly built. Soon the barn was completely surrounded by Union cavalry, and Detective Baker ordered the men to come out. "Never! Come in and get me!" replied the defiant Booth, who then offered to come out and fight if the troopers would back away fifty paces. The soldiers were ordered to gather and lay straw along the base of the barn and to prepare to fire the building.

While Booth continued to yell challenges at his besiegers, his accomplice, Herold, was begging Booth to give up. Booth called out to the detectives, "The young man who is with me will surrender." Doherty opened the barn door slightly to allow Herold to come out, at which point the cavalry officer slammed the door and tackled Herold. Booth's companion was tied to a tree, and Millington was posted to guard him. Millington asked Herold if the man in the barn was Booth, and Herold confirmed that it was. Herold then told Millington that he had no knowledge that Booth had planned to kill the president. Their plan was to kidnap Lincoln and hold him hostage until Union troops withdrew from the South. Herold cried to Millington that he had fallen under Booth's spell and that after the assassination, Booth had threatened to kill him if he did not help him escape. Herold was laying out to Millington the basis of his defense at his upcoming conspiracy trial. Millington, the hardened war veteran, was unmoved by Herold's pleas, as was the military tribunal that condemned Herold.

As Herold confessed to Millington, the order was given to set fire to the barn. As the orange flames illuminated the interior of the barn, Parady and the other men could see Booth scurrying about, trying to stomp out the flames, but his broken leg rendered the attempt futile. The detectives planned to take Booth alive by jumping him as he fled the fire, but that chance never came. The situation at the barn was practically a mob scene, with many of the soldiers bent on revenge. From his position guarding Herold, Millington could hear the soldiers yelling for Booth to show himself. Sergeant Boston Corbett, seeing through vents in the barn that Booth was armed with a Spencer rifle, fired one shot from his Colt revolver. The ball struck Booth in the neck and dropped him to the ground. The troopers rushed inside the flaming structure and dragged the unconscious Booth outside, laying him on the Garretts' front porch.

Parady and the men surrounded Booth as he regained consciousness. Paralyzed from the bullet, Booth asked to see his hands, and when the soldiers raised his arms for him to see, Booth muttered, "Useless." Booth lived about two hours after being shot, the grisly death scene lit by lanterns and the fire from the barn. His last words were "Tell Mother I died for my country." Booth's body was wrapped in an army blanket and placed in a wagon. As the sun rose in Virginia, the soldiers, detectives, their prisoners and the wagon with Booth's body drove to the river, where the steamer that had brought them waited for their return. On the journey, in return for his collaboration, Willie Jett was allowed to "escape." On board ship, Herold was placed in a cabin, and again Millington was detailed to guard him while another soldier was stationed outside the door. Upon his relief, Millington, frigid because he had no overcoat, made his way to the ship's boiler room to sleep where it was warm.

When the boat reached the Washington Navy Yard, the docks were jammed with people. When Booth had been shot, Detective Conger had gone ahead of the men and sent word to the War Department of the capture.

The dying murderer drawn from the barn where he had taken refuge. *Library of Congress.*

The news had gotten out, and thousands had turned out to see the body or at least congratulate the captors. Because of the curious throngs, Doherty decided not to try to take Booth's corpse ashore. He ordered Millington and others to move the body and place it on the deck of an ironclad navy warship. With their duty complete, Doherty, Millington, Parady and their comrades returned to their barracks for a hot meal and a sound sleep. When they awoke the next day, the papers had long articles about the killing of Booth and the capture of Herold.

The end of the Civil War brought a return to civilian life for the men of the 16th New York Cavalry. Emory Parady received his discharge in May 1865 and headed for home. John Millington had one final duty: twenty members of the 16th New York were present at the July 7, 1865 hanging of David Herold and three co-conspirators of the Lincoln assassination.

Soldiers Share Reward Money

Millington mustered out of the cavalry when the regiment was disbanded in September. Like Parady, Millington returned to upstate New York and his parents' farm. He married shortly after returning home and began a family.

About a year after the death of Booth and the execution of Herold, the U.S. government paid out $100,000.00 in reward money to those persons who played a role in the capture of the assassination conspirators. Each of the twenty-six enlisted men of the 16th New York received $1,658.58, the equivalent of ten years of army pay.

Millington used $800 of his reward to buy a farm near Chester, New York, but like many Civil War veterans, he headed west. By 1875, he and his wife, Phoebe, were farming near Summit Lake, Minnesota. Parady moved west with his parents and settled near Berlin, Michigan. He married a girl from Ohio, and by 1870, Emory and his bride, Frances, had invested his reward money and owned a farm valued at $1,700. The Paradys grew

Emory Parady. *Courtesy of Steven G. Miller.*

tired of simple farming life, and by 1880 they had relocated to Nashville Village in Michigan, where Emory worked as a cobbler operating his own shoe business. Parady prospered in Nashville Village, serving as postmaster from 1881 to 1886, a time when post office boxes rented for forty cents per year. He was also elected to a term as village president. Emory and Frances Parady made Michigan their home for thirty years before moving to Oregon. The couple raised two sons, Silas and Albert, and three daughters, Elizabeth, Nellie and Blanche.

John Millington also gave up farming to pursue a trade. He became a carpenter and moved his family from Minnesota to Sioux City, Iowa. John and Phoebe raised five sons: John Jr., Joseph, James, George and Benjamin. Phoebe died after the turn of the century, and John took his carpentry skills to Portland, where his sons George and Joseph lived.

Parady brought his business to Portland sometime between 1901 and 1908. Portland census records list Parady as a shoemaker and show daughters Elizabeth and Nellie working in a photography gallery and living with their father and mother. In Oregon, Parady was reunited with his old saddle-mate Millington. Both of the Civil War veterans, now gray and in their sixties, were members of Portland's Benjamin F. Butler Post 67 of the GAR. Following a three-year battle with cancer, John W. Millington died on November 11, 1914. He was seventy-one. Emory Parady died at age eighty at his Portland home on March 14, 1924.

FINAL RESTING PLACES

President Abraham Lincoln is buried in Springfield, Illinois, beneath a magnificent 117-foot-tall tomb. He is immortalized around the world, from Lincoln Memorial to Mount Rushmore, and also with a 10-foot-tall statue in downtown Portland. Booth rots in an unmarked grave in his family's plot in Baltimore. John Millington is buried at the Grand Army of the Republic Cemetery in southwest Portland. His grave is marked by a simple veteran's headstone. Emory Parady, fittingly, rests in Lincoln Memorial Park in east Portland. His distinctive granite monument reads: "Member Co. H, 16th NY Cavalry. One of the twenty-six enlisted men who captured John Wilkes Booth, assassin of President Abraham Lincoln."

One Blast Upon Your Bugle

An Oregon Senator Makes the Ultimate Sacrifice

Edward Dickinson Baker was at the height of political power. The senior senator from the newly admitted state of Oregon was a close personal friend and confidant of the president. Despite status and privilege, the life of the veteran politician was destined to end on a blood-soaked field along the banks of the Potomac River.

Baker, fifty years old and known to his friends as Ned, was of average height with a bit of a paunch. Balding, what hair he had left was now white. His parents brought him from London to Philadelphia when he was five years old. Baker's father, also named Edward, was a schoolteacher, and he moved his family to Indiana and then to the Illinois frontier when young Ned was a teenager. The junior Baker met territorial governor Ninian Edwards, who took a liking to him and allowed the young man access to the governor's private law library. Baker taught himself the law and was admitted to the Illinois bar at the age of nineteen.

After serving in the Black Hawk War of 1832, Baker married a widow with two children and established a law practice in Springfield, Illinois. Ned and Mary Ann Baker would have four more children. In Springfield, Baker became acquainted with another self-educated country lawyer named Abraham Lincoln. The two men became fast friends and enmeshed themselves in the politics of their day. Baker served in the Illinois House of Representatives and later the state senate. In 1844, both Baker and Lincoln sought the Whig Party's nomination for Congress. Baker received the nomination and won the general election. His victory over his colleague did not strain their friendship: Lincoln named his second son Edward Baker Lincoln.

Senator
Edward D.
Baker. *Library of
Congress.*

Congressman Baker was still in his first term of office when the United
States went to war with Mexico. Baker resigned his congressional seat to
accept an army commission as colonel of Illinois volunteers. He served
gallantly in the siege of Veracruz and commanded a brigade under
General Winfield Scott at Cerro Gordo. Baker returned to Springfield a
war hero, but in the colonel's absence, Lincoln had been elected to Baker's
congressional seat. Rather than politically challenge his friend again, Baker
relocated to Galena, Illinois, where in 1848 he was elected to Congress
from that district. Lincoln lost in his bid for reelection.

The ever-ambitious Baker did not seek reelection in 1850 because he expected to receive a cabinet appointment from President Fillmore. When his dream of a greater position did not materialize, Baker packed his bags and joined the Gold Rush to California. He set up a law practice in San Francisco and became a leader in the new Republican Party but was unsuccessful in winning one of the Golden State's senate seats. When Lincoln received the Republican nomination for president in 1860, Baker threw himself behind his friend's campaign.

Baker traveled extensively up and down the Pacific coast speaking on behalf of Honest Abe. When Baker was campaigning in Oregon, which had a vacant U.S. Senate seat, local politicians enticed him to move his family to Salem. Oregon Republicans sought to exploit a split in the Democratic majority, which was divided between supporters of Illinois senator Stephen A. Douglas and followers of Oregon's proslavery senator, Joseph Lane. Baker rented a house on the campus of Willamette University, and with support from Douglas Democrats, the state legislature elected Baker to the Senate in October 1860. Baker had realized his dream. He was the first Republican senator from the West Coast. A month later, due greatly to Baker's efforts, Lincoln carried both Oregon and California and was elected the sixteenth president of the United States. At Lincoln's inauguration ceremony, the man chosen to introduce the president-elect to the audience was Senator Edward D. Baker of Oregon.

THE SENATOR RAISES A REGIMENT

At the outbreak of hostilities, Baker volunteered for military service. He was offered a commission as brigadier general, but at that rank he would be required to resign from the Senate. Baker expected the war to be short-lived, and he was not about to give up his long-coveted Senate seat. Instead, he accepted a commission as colonel of U.S. volunteers. Colonel Baker performed double duty as soldier and senator. An advocate for vigorous prosecution of the war, Baker personally recruited a regiment of infantry and outfitted the troops at his own expense. He mustered his 1,600 men primarily from Philadelphia and New York but was also joined by volunteers from California and Oregon. Unlike other volunteer regiments, Baker's men were considered part of the Regular Army. Baker deemed that their numbers would count toward California's enlistment quota, and the senator from Oregon dubbed his regiment the 1st California Volunteers.

Baker often appeared in the Senate wearing his military uniform. *Library of Congress.*

A few days after the Confederate victory at Bull Run, Kentucky senator and former vice president John C. Breckenridge took the Senate floor to defend secession and to condemn the use of military force against Southern states. Baker had been away from the Senate that day drilling with his troops and arrived in the chamber as Breckenridge was speaking. Baker was wearing his blue uniform coat, carrying his forage cap in one hand and a riding crop in the other hand as he strode to his chair. As he waited for Breckenridge to finish his remarks, the senator/soldier unbuckled his sword and laid it across his desk. Baker launched into an impromptu and unrehearsed defense of the Union, the president and the Federal army and a scathing rebuke and condemnation of secession. Baker's oratorical skills were enhanced by his striking martial manifestation. He waxed eloquently about Rome, Hannibal, the attack on Fort Sumter and the evils of slavery. He called Breckenridge an apologist for treason and vowed to subjugate the rebellious states by force and compel their obedience to the Constitution. Baker's discourse made national headlines and is remembered as one of the most dramatic addresses ever delivered in Congress. Later that year, Breckenridge was expelled from the Senate and went on to become a Confederate general.

DESTINY AT BALL'S BLUFF

Colonel Baker spent his last Sunday visiting the White House. He had dined with the Lincoln family on the lawn and discussed the course of the war. General McClellan had ordered Baker's brigade to march to the Potomac for a reconnaissance of the Leesburg area, and Baker informed the president that he would join his men in the field the next day. He bid a late afternoon farewell to his friend.

As dawn broke on Monday, October 21, 1861, Baker left Washington for the front. The Potomac River at Leesburg runs wide and deep. A two-mile-long landmass, Harrison's Island, splits the channel, creating a bottleneck that hindered advance and retreat. At dawn, 350 men of the 15th Massachusetts Infantry crossed from the Maryland side to the island by boat, marched the four hundred yards across the island and again boarded boats to cross to the Virginia side of the river.

On the Virginia bank is a shale and sandstone cliff known as Ball's Bluff, which stands eighty-five feet above the river with a meandering cart path leading from the riverbank to the top, which featured a large meadow-like clearing, about ten acres in size, surrounded by heavy woods. The Union crossing was unopposed, and the men formed up in the clearing and sent out pickets to determine if the Confederates had abandoned the area. About eight o'clock that morning, the pickets ran into and engaged men of the 17th Mississippi Regiment. The Battle of Ball's Bluff had begun.

When Baker arrived at General Charles P. Stone's headquarters, Stone ordered him to cross the river and take command of the troops. Baker was to assess the situation and either advance toward Leesburg or withdraw back across the Potomac. Stone sent a telegraph to McClellan in Washington that Baker had crossed into Virginia and was advancing on Leesburg. Stone advised that he felt he could occupy Leesburg by nightfall. He concluded his message with: "We are a little short of boats." President Lincoln was informed of the fighting and hurried to McClellan's headquarters to monitor messages from the front.

As Baker arrived at the river, he met a Union courier and was informed of the fighting. Without assessing his position, Baker immediately began organizing all available boats and ordered as many men as he could find to cross the river. The 20th Massachusetts was followed by Baker's own California Brigade.

The Confederates began sending reinforcements to the bluff as well. Colonel Nathan Evans ordered two companies of Virginia cavalry and a company of the 18th Mississippi Infantry to join the mêlée. He then called for the 8th Virginia to march to the fight. When Baker arrived on the bluff, he sent the 1st California forward to find the enemy's flank. They ran headlong into the Virginians. A sharp exchange of musket volleys concluded with both sides falling back to regroup. The Confederate defenders continued to fire from the woods while Baker kept his men in the clearing, recklessly exposing his men and himself to enemy musket balls. When Baker recognized the Tammany Regiment from New York City arriving to reinforce him, he waved his cap at their colonel and greeted him with a shouted quote from Sir Walter Scott: "One blast upon your bugle horn is worth a thousand men!"

At that point, each army had 1,700 men crowded onto the bluff, and although the forces were equal in number, the defenders had tactical advantage. Thick woods surrounded the clearing, and red, yellow and orange leaves clung to the trees, camouflaging the position and movement of the Confederates. The Federals had hauled three artillery pieces up the steep path and deployed them in the clearing. The big guns proved ineffective because Confederate marksmen hidden in the woods picked off the gunners. Infantrymen from the 1st California took over manning the cannon, and at one point even Baker himself was helping push the guns into position. The two smaller pieces, mountain howitzers, were abandoned, but Baker continued to personally direct fire from a bronze thirteen-pounder James rifled cannon. At about 4:30 p.m., the Confederates unleashed a deadly musket volley. Baker was struck simultaneously in the chest, neck and head by at least four balls. The poetry-quoting colonel was killed instantly. The Rebels closed on the Federals, and desperate hand-to-hand combat whirled about Baker's body as his men fought to keep his remains from falling to the enemy and carried their commander to the boats.

With Baker down, the Union troops began a wild retreat, and the shortage of boats proved fatal. Overloaded vessels capsized, and men drowned attempting to swim the river. For weeks after the battle, bodies of Union soldiers washed up on the riverbanks at Washington.

Of the 1,700 Union soldiers who crossed the river into Virginia, nearly 1,000 were killed, wounded, missing or captured. Among the men captured that day was Major Paul J. Revere of Boston, grandson of the Patriot. Among the wounded was Lieutenant Oliver Wendell Holmes, a future Supreme Court justice.

The Confederates lost 36 killed and 117 wounded. The dead of the victorious Confederates were sent home to their families. The Union dead left on the field were buried the next day under a flag of truce. A small national cemetery now stands on the bluff. Within the cemetery, enclosed by

Federal soldiers battle to keep Baker's body from the enemy. *Library of Congress.*

a stone wall, lie the remains of 54 Union soldiers who perished during the Battle of Ball's Bluff.

At McClellan's headquarters in Washington, the general himself informed President Lincoln of Baker's death and the Union defeat. Lincoln was so upset by the news that he left immediately, almost collapsing as he stepped into the street. Lincoln's ten-year-old son, Willie, wrote a poem in tribute to Baker.

Baker's death shocked the nation and led to the formation of a Congressional Joint Committee on the Conduct of the War. The colonel's body lay in state in the Senate chamber. Mary Lincoln created a minor scandal by wearing a lilac dress to his funeral. The First Lady retorted, "I wonder if the women of Washington expect me to muffle myself in mourning for every soldier killed in this Great War?" Memorial services were held throughout Oregon and California. Senator Baker's body was transported to California, where he is interred, overlooking San Francisco Bay, in the National Cemetery at the Presidio.

GONE BUT NOT FORGOTTEN

Oregonians named Baker City and Baker County in honor of their fallen hero. Life-sized marble statues of Edward D. Baker stand in the rotunda of

The Baker monument at Ball's Bluff identifies Baker as the colonel of the 71st Pennsylvania Infantry, but Baker's regiment was not adopted by Pennsylvania until after the senator's death. *Photo by Karen Fletcher.*

the U.S. Capitol and in the statehouse in Sacramento. A painting depicting the Battle of Ball's Bluff hangs in the White House.

Baker has also received honors from descendants of Civil War veterans. The Colonel Edward D. Baker Camp of the Sons of Union Veterans of the Civil War is based in Oregon. To commemorate the bicentennial of Baker's birth (February 24, 1811), the Oregon legislature passed Senate Bill 809, which designates every February 24 as Edward D. Baker Day in Oregon.

The battlefield at Ball's Bluff is now preserved and is posted with numerous historical markers. A short distance outside the stone walls of the national cemetery stand two small monuments. One is a granite tribute to Virginian Clinton Hatcher, who "fell bravely defending his native state." Legend has it that long after the war, Massachusetts veterans visiting Ball's Bluff inquired about a tall flag-bearer who was cut down in the battle's final charge. Upon learning Hatcher's identity and his fate, the men of the Bay State commissioned and shipped a carved block of black Quincy granite to Leesburg to honor Hatcher's gallantry.

About one hundred yards from the Hatcher memorial is a small marble stone, the size and shape used to mark the graves of Confederate soldiers. Its engraving states "Col. Edward D. Baker killed here." The monuments allegedly mark the exact locations where the courageous warriors fell.

Although neither Hatcher nor Baker is buried there, visitors to the battlefield sometimes mistakenly believe that the stones mark the graves of the men. Even former secretary of state George C. Marshall was fooled. The great statesman and soldier lived in Leesburg, and he was walking the battlefield one summer day in 1949 when he stumbled across the Baker marker, which was overgrown with brush. Marshall believed the spot to be Baker's grave and commented on his discovery to President Truman, who, in typical "Give 'em Hell Harry" fashion, decided to take matters into his own hands. Truman summoned Oregon senator Wayne Morse to the White House, and the thirty-third president of the United States drove Morse thirty-five miles from Washington to Leesburg. There they met General Marshall and cleared the brush away from the Baker stone, only to discover that it was not Baker's grave. This may have been the last time a sitting U.S. president drove a car on public roads.

Before the O.K. Corral

How the Civil War Brought Virgil Earp to Portland

On an autumn afternoon in 1881, four armed lawmen strode down a dusty street in Tombstone. They headed toward the O.K. Corral and immortality. The leader of the quartet was Virgil Earp, serving a dual capacity as Tombstone city marshal and deputy U.S. marshal for the Arizona Territory. Accompanying Virgil were his younger brother Morgan, who was his regular city deputy, and two other men specially deputized for that day: Wyatt Earp and Doc Holliday.

The lawmen were on their way to arrest members of the Cowboys, an outlaw faction notorious for rustling and robbery. The Cowboy offense that day was carrying firearms within city limits in violation of a Tombstone ordinance. A long series of events had led to the bloody confrontation that was about to erupt, and details of the conflict are readily available in print and on film.

Upon reaching an alley near the O.K. Corral, Virgil Earp and his bold deputies confronted five members of the Cowboys. Virgil hoped to avoid a fight and carried Doc Holliday's cane in his gun hand. He commanded the Cowboys to throw up their hands, but gunfire broke out immediately. To this day, there is dispute over who fired the first shot. Some claim it was Doc Holliday, while others say that Doc fired in response to Cowboy Billy Clanton drawing his pistol. In any case, the hail of lead that followed lasted less than thirty seconds. When the shooting was over, three of the Cowboys lay dead in the street: Billy Clanton, Tom McLaury and Frank McLaury. The other two Cowboys, Ike Clanton and Billy Claiborne, were able to run away unhurt. Morgan Earp was wounded in his back above his shoulder blades. Virgil was shot through the calf of his right leg, and Doc Holliday was hit in the hip. Wyatt Earp came out of the gunfight unscathed.

EARP BROTHERS GROW UP IN ILLINOIS AND IOWA

Nicholas and Virginia Earp were farmers who raised a family of seven boys and four girls. Originally from Hartford, Kentucky, they later moved to Monmouth, Illinois, and Pella, Iowa. Virgil Walter Earp, their third son, was born on July 18, 1843. At the age of sixteen, Virgil eloped with a Dutch girl named Ellen Rysdam, who was also just sixteen. Virgil and Ellen would have a daughter, Nellie Jane.

When the Civil War began, the eldest Earp boys volunteered to fight for the Union. Oldest son James volunteered with the 17th Illinois Infantry and was discharged after being badly wounded at Fredericktown. Newton served as a sergeant in the 4th Iowa Cavalry and fought at Vicksburg. Virgil served in the 83rd Illinois Infantry. The rest of the Earp brothers, including Wyatt and Morgan, were too young for military service.

Private Virgil Earp was still a teenager when he marched off to war, leaving behind his wife and a two-week-old baby girl. He would not see his wife or daughter again for thirty-seven years because in the summer of 1863, his wife was told that Earp had been killed in Tennessee. Heartbroken, Ellen took her daughter and headed

Virgil and Allie Earp in Arizona. *Courtesy of Mike Utley and Cheryl Johnson.*

west with her parents. Unaware of the reports of his death, Earp served throughout the Civil War, seeing action in Tennessee and Kentucky under General George Thomas. By the end of the war, the 83rd Illinois had lost 121 men and officers. Virgil Earp was not among the dead; he returned home in the summer of 1865, three years after he left, to find his wife and baby gone and no way to contact them.

Like tens of thousands of Civil War veterans, the Earp brothers headed west for a fresh start and new opportunities. For the next decade, Virgil moved around the country, holding various jobs such as farming, railroad construction and stagecoach driving. He married, divorced and married again. The Earps were a tightknit family who kept in close contact with one another and often ventured into business as a family. Virgil spent time in Dodge City, where younger brother Wyatt served with Bat Masterson as deputy city marshals.

In 1877, Virgil and his third wife, a diminutive beauty named Allie Sullivan, moved to Prescott, Arizona, where Virgil became deputy sheriff for Yavapai County. It was in Prescott that Virgil was involved in his first street gunfight, killing an outlaw with a shot from a Winchester rifle. Afterward, Virgil won election as Prescott town constable.

BROTHERS REUNITED IN TOMBSTONE

In 1879, Virgil's experience in law enforcement and his Republican political persuasion earned him an appointment as deputy U.S. marshal. He was assigned to the southern portion of Arizona Territory and chose Tombstone as his residence. There he was reunited with brothers Wyatt and James, who were running a saloon and stage business and speculating on a silver mine. The next year, brothers Morgan and Warren also moved to Tombstone.

Following the gunfight at the O.K. Corral, Ike Clanton filed murder charges against the three Earp brothers and Doc Holliday. A trial was held, with the judge ruling that the four defendants had acted within the scope of the law, and the charges were dismissed. Thwarted in court, the Cowboys sought other opportunities for revenge.

Three nights after Christmas 1881, Virgil Earp was walking alone on Tombstone's Allen Street when he was hit by a shotgun blast. The buckshot tore through his left arm and into his side and crippled Earp's arm for life. Even as the doctors worked to save his life, Earp told his wife, Allie, "Never mind, I've got one good arm left to hug you with." Three months later, Morgan Earp was killed while playing billiards. He was ambushed and shot in the back.

Wyatt Earp. *Author's collection.*

Older brother James Earp escorted Morgan's body to their parents' home in California for burial. Virgil and Allie Earp were sent to Tucson so that he could recover from his wounds in safety. Wyatt Earp was appointed U.S. marshal, with authority to name his own deputies. Wyatt, along with brother Warren, Doc Holliday and other deputies, embarked on a vendetta to exterminate the Cowboys from Arizona. The events of 1881 and 1882 are portrayed in the motion picture *Tombstone* starring Kurt Russell as Wyatt Earp, with Virgil heroically portrayed by Sam Elliott.

It took Virgil two full years to recover from his gunshot wounds. Once he was well enough to leave Tucson, he traveled to his parents' home in Colton, California. The gunfight at the O.K. Corral had made the Earps famous, and Virgil, despite having the use of just one arm, was hired as a special guard by Southern Pacific Railroad. When Colton became an incorporated city in 1887, Earp was elected as its first city marshal and was paid a salary of seventy-five dollars a month. Virgil and Allie stayed on the move for the next twenty-five years, living at times in California, Colorado, Arizona and Nevada. They occasionally visited his brother Wyatt and his other siblings and engaged in a number of business ventures, including mining, saloon keeping and ranching. Virgil was famous wherever he went and often worked in law enforcement.

A LETTER ARRIVES FROM OREGON

Virgil was again living in Prescott, Arizona, when he received a letter from Mrs. Levi Law of Portland. Mrs. Law was in fact his long-lost daughter,

Nellie Jane. The exploits of Wyatt and Virgil Earp and Doc Holliday had been published in newspapers and dime novels throughout the United States and even Europe. Virgil's fame reached Portland, where his first wife, Ellen, still believing Virgil had perished in the Civil War, was remarried and residing with her new husband and her daughter by Virgil. Allie and Virgil Earp had no children, and it was Allie who encouraged Virgil to travel to Portland to meet his only child.

Earp visited his daughter and the Rose City in the spring of 1899. There, for the first time, he met the three grandchildren he never knew existed. The *Oregonian* reported on the visit of the famous lawman. Even in his late fifties, Virgil Earp was an imposing figure of a man, tall and broad shouldered. Years later, Earp's grandson, George Law, would tell of a lesson he learned from the old marshal. The family went for a ride on one of Portland's streetcars, but before boarding, Grandpa Earp told the kids, "I'm not going to give the conductor my fare." The family took their seats, and the conductor came down the aisle to collect a nickel from each passenger. When the conductor came to where Earp was sitting, he didn't stop or ask for Virgil's five cents; he just kept moving down the aisle. Asked by his daughter why the conductor didn't collect his fare, Earp replied, "It's the way I looked at him. He was afraid of the look." Having finished the demonstration for his grandchildren, Earp stopped as he exited the streetcar and paid the conductor the required fare. The year after Earp's trip to Portland, Nellie Jane made the trip to Arizona to visit her father and Allie.

In 1904, Virgil and Allie Earp moved to Goldfield, Nevada, to join Wyatt in speculating on a gold strike. Virgil was appointed deputy sheriff of Esmeralda County, the final post in his law enforcement career. The next year, Virgil contracted pneumonia, and on October 19, 1905, one of the most colorful figures of the American West passed into history. He was sixty-two years old. At the request of his daughter, Nellie Jane, Allie allowed Virgil's remains to be sent to Portland for burial. Allie lived another forty-two years but never remarried. Virgil was the love of her life. She moved to California, where she lived with members of the Earp family. Allie Earp died at the age of ninety-nine and is buried in Los Angeles next to her best friend, Virgil's sister Adelia Earp Edwards.

River View Cemetery is located on Macadam Boulevard in southwest Portland. In section fifteen of the cemetery, beneath a variegated holly tree, rest the remains of U.S. marshal Virgil W. Earp. His headstone is quite unpretentious: a gray granite tube-shaped marker set low to the ground. There is no mention of his Civil War service, his career as a lawman, the

O.K. Corral or his famous brother Wyatt. His epitaph reads simply: "God will take care of me." His daughter, Nellie Jane, is buried with her family in a nearby plot. A spokesman for the cemetery reports that of all the people buried in the cemetery, Virgil Earp is the most asked-about grave.

The Professors in Pickett's Charge

Pioneers of Oregon Higher Education Fought at Gettysburg

It was hot and muggy. Captain Hawthorne was damp in his gray wool uniform as he stood close by his brigade commander and waited for the order to advance. Hawthorne had been given the honor of serving on the general's personal staff. The sky was mostly sunny, but thunderheads rose in the distance. The temperature stood at eighty-seven degrees on that Pennsylvania summer day, but the humidity and the damp wool made it feel as if it were over one hundred degrees.

It was loud, too. Ungodly loud! Nearly two hundred cannon had roared for an earth-shaking hour as the afternoon approached two o'clock. Ben Arnold had been a student in his native Virginia, but today he was a soldier hearing the bellow of cannon. His regiment had formed up between a peach orchard and a line of cannons that was pounding the Union position. From where he was positioned, Arnold could not see his classmate B.J. Hawthorne, but he knew Hawthorne would be up front, close by the general.

Hawthorne and Arnold were soldiers in Lewis Armistead's infantry brigade, part of the all-Virginian division commanded by Confederate general George E. Pickett. It was July 3, 1863, and in a few moments, they would step into history: Pickett's Charge at Gettysburg.

The two Virginia college alumni survived the day that took the lives of thousands of their comrades. Though their escape would not be unscathed, they would live to teach together ten years later and 2,700 miles away in Corvallis, where they would chart the course of Oregon State University.

Prior to the Civil War, George Pickett served in the Oregon Territory. When Virginia seceded, he resigned from the army to join the Confederacy. *Library of Congress.*

COLLEGE CLASSMATES ENLIST

Benjamin Lee Arnold and Benjamin James Hawthorne had known each other at Randolph Macon College. Both were graduates of the class of 1861, with Arnold, age twenty-one, earning his degree in philosophy and religion and Hawthorne, three years older than Arnold, receiving his master's in romance languages. Both men were from Mecklenburg County, Virginia, and upon graduation, they joined the Confederate army together. They enlisted in the

38th Virginia Infantry Regiment, Company G, known as the Mecklenburg Rifles. Hawthorne was elected as the company's lieutenant, while Arnold was chosen to be a sergeant. Sergeant Arnold's enlistment in the 38th lasted just three months before he received a disability discharge due to injury.

Arnold recovered from the injury that forced him out of the regiment and reenlisted in an artillery unit before transferring to the 14th Virginia Infantry. He was assigned to Company F, the Chambliss Grays, and was reunited with Hawthorne a year later when the 14th and 38th Regiments were assigned to Armistead's Brigade. Hawthorne was promoted to captain and was the commander of Company G until just before Gettysburg, when Armistead requested his service on the brigade staff.

Just after two o'clock on that sweltering July afternoon, the cannons ceased fire. The silence seemed as deafening as the roar of the guns, but the quiet lasted only a few moments before it was broken by the beat of drums and the shouting of officers. Hawthorne, Arnold and all of Pickett's Division were moved forward in front of the now silent artillery and formed in a battle line on the edge of an open expanse of fields. The Confederate battle line stretched almost a mile from one end to the other—12,500 infantry dressed in gray and butternut brown. Pickett's 4,000 Virginians were in the center of the line. Bayonets were fixed, flags unfurled and men waited for the order to advance. A moment frozen in history. On the other side of the field, three-quarters of a mile away and clearly visible, was the enemy line at the foot of Cemetery Ridge.

Eyewitnesses to the Confederate formation described it as the most beautiful sight they had ever seen, rows upon rows of bayonets gleaming in the sun. Never again would the flower of the Southern military tradition be arrayed in such glory. William Faulkner, the quintessential southern novelist, wrote of that exact moment eighty-five years later:

> For every Southern boy fourteen years old, not once but whenever he wants it, there is the instant when it's still not yet two o'clock on that July afternoon in 1863, the brigades are in position behind the rail fence, the guns are laid and ready in the woods and the furled flags are already loosened to break out and Pickett himself with his long oiled ringlets and his hat in one hand probably and his sword in the other looking up the hill waiting for Longstreet to give the word and it's all in the balance, it hasn't happened yet, it hasn't even begun yet, it not only hasn't begun yet but there is still time for it not to begin against that position and those circumstances which made more men than Garnett and Kemper and Armistead and Wilcox look grave

yet it's going to begin, we all know that, we have come too far with too much at stake and that moment doesn't need even a fourteen-year-old boy to think This time. Maybe this time with all this much to lose and all this much to gain: Pennsylvania, Maryland, the world, the golden dome of Washington itself to crown with desperate and unbelievable victory the desperate gamble, the cast made two years ago.

The order to advance was given, and the line of men in gray with their scarlet battle flags moved out at a marching pace in a parade-like order, shoulder to shoulder. Armistead's Brigade, including Hawthorne and Arnold, was in the second line of battle, arranged to plug any gaps that might open. As the Confederates advanced, the Union held its fire until the men in gray reached the Emmitsburg Road, halfway point of the assault. At that point, Yankee artillery opened fire. Barrages from Union guns positioned on Little Round Top forced back the divisions on Pickett's right flank, exposing his men to attack. A Vermont brigade moving quickly exploited the opening on the flank and opened fire on the side and back of Pickett's Division, decimating them with withering musket fire. Still the Virginians pressed onward, with Armistead leading the attack, his hat on the end of his sword. As they approached the enemy, Union artillery loaded double canister, hundreds of round balls that turned their cannons into giant shotguns. On command, eleven cannon and 1,700 Union muskets fired at once. Entire regiments disappeared. Historian Shelby Foote described that instant: "When those cannon discharged some southern towns just did not have young men anymore." Arnold's regiment was repulsed by brutal combat with men of the 19th Massachusetts. Arnold's colonel, major and adjutant were all killed. Seven out of the ten company commanders were killed, wounded or captured, and the regiment was forced to retreat. Arnold made his way back to safety, but it is not known whether he was wounded or not.

Farther up the Confederate line, Armistead's brigade charged with bayonets and forced the Federal troops to fall back. The general himself, with troops including Hawthorne's regiment, climbed over a low stone wall, where the barrier made a ninety-degree turn known as the Angle. They seized some of the Union cannon positioned behind the wall. In a little less than ten minutes of hand-to-hand fighting, with rifle butts and bayonets the weapons of expediency, every man in the vicinity of the Angle, blue and gray, was killed, wounded or captured. Hawthorne was shot down before he reached the wall. Armistead was personally attempting to turn a cannon around to fire on the retreating enemy when he was shot. The Philadelphia

The soldiers in Pickett's Charge had to cross nearly a mile of open terrain under Union artillery and musket fire. *Photo by author.*

brigade re-formed and countercharged the Confederates, retaking the wall and capturing the battle flag of Hawthorne's 38th Virginia Regiment. Hawthorne himself, though badly wounded, was able to retreat back across the field as his friend Arnold had done. Armistead was taken captive and died of his wounds.

The whole fight was over in less than an hour. The farthest advance of Armistead's brigade into the Union line is known as the "High-Water Mark of the Confederacy." Of the twelve thousand Confederate soldiers who began the assault, fewer than half made it back to safety. Pickett was devastated. When Robert E. Lee encountered Pickett after the battle, he ordered him to see to his division. Pickett replied, "General Lee, I have no division." At six o'clock in the evening, the thunderclouds that Hawthorne had noticed earlier in the day moved in and dumped rain on the blood-soaked fields. The sound of the thunder seemed muted compared to the roar of cannons, but the Battle of Gettysburg had ended. The wagons carrying the Confederate wounded stretched for seventeen miles.

Following Gettysburg, Hawthorne recovered from his wounds and returned to command Company G of the 38th Virginia. Pickett's Division was never as effective as it had been before the famous charge. On April 9, 1865, Lee surrendered to Grant at Appomattox Court House. The

Chambliss Grays, Arnold's unit, was the largest company left in the 14th Virginia. Ten of its one hundred men were able to report for duty. Hawthorne's regiment surrendered with just seventy-three men. Grant's terms of surrender allowed the defeated Rebels to keep their horses, but soldiers confiscated Hawthorne's mount anyway, and he was forced to walk back home.

Upon returning home, Hawthorne married, began raising a family and moved to Louisiana to teach romance languages at the Collegiate Institute in Baton Rouge. Hawthorne and his wife, Emma, would have two sons, Edgar and Wistar, and a daughter named after her mother. Arnold also married and started a family, but his wife, Addie, died and left him a widower with a four-year-old son. Arnold left his son, Harry, with his wife's family in Virginia and took a job teaching at West Tennessee College, where he distinguished himself as a professor of mathematics and natural science.

When struggling Corvallis College in Oregon needed a new president in the summer of 1872, the bishops of the Methodist Episcopal Church South asked Professor Arnold to go west. President Arnold changed the name of Corvallis College to Corvallis State Agricultural College and then to Oregon Agricultural College. Arnold would serve as president of the college for twenty years and remains a giant figure in the history of Oregon State

OAC faculty in 1887. President Benjamin Arnold is third from the left; Professor B.J. Hawthorne is third from the right. *Courtesy OSU Archives.*

University. Early in his tenure, Arnold asked his army colleague Hawthorne to join the faculty. Hawthorne accepted the offer and made the journey from Louisiana to Oregon by wagon in 1874.

During Arnold's administration, he introduced the study of scientific agriculture at the school and authorized experiments for the purpose of helping farmers in the state. Faculty and students spent eight hours a day in the classroom and were required to work on the college's farm during after-school hours. The college was organized into two departments subdivided into different schools, with a faculty member heading each department. Arnold also established an alumni association for the school and introduced intercollegiate athletics when he allowed the formation of a baseball team, breaking the long-standing tradition in which debate was the only authorized student social activity allowed outside the classroom.

EX-CONFEDERATES ON CORVALLIS CAMPUS

Arnold introduced military science to the curriculum and hired an active-duty army officer to lead the cadet corps. This precursor to the modern ROTC was the first instance in the United States of a commissioned officer serving on a college campus as a professor of military science while still on active duty. When the army reassigned its officer to another post, ex-soldiers Hawthorne and Arnold personally drilled the cadet corps. The uniforms, chosen by Arnold, were Confederate gray.

Hawthorne quickly became the star of the OAC faculty. As the first chairman of the Agriculture Department, he taught horticulture and botany and collected, tested and museum-mounted seeds, grasses, fruits and injurious pests. He also taught zoology, care of domestic animals and stockbreeding. In addition to Arnold and Hawthorne, a number of other early leaders of OAC had Confederate connections. Among them were mathematics professor John Letcher, the son of Virginia's Civil War governor, and Reverend J.R.N. Bell, a member of the Board of Regents and a veteran of the 26th Virginia Infantry.

Among Arnold's accomplishments as president was to move the campus from Fifth Street to the present location of OSU. He supervised the fundraising and construction of the first college building on the new site, today's Benton Hall. President Arnold fell in love with and married one of his students, Minnie White. After his marriage, Arnold sent for his son Harry in Virginia, and the two were reunited after an eight-year separation.

Arnold would father another son, Ernest, with his new wife. Both of the Arnold sons would graduate from OAC.

In 1892, Arnold fell ill while speaking to the Oregon Senate in Salem. He was rushed home on a special train arranged by the governor but died at his Corvallis home on January 30. He was just fifty-two years old, but his twenty years as president are the second-longest tenure of any president in the history of Oregon State University. President Arnold's epitaph is written on a bronze tablet on the second floor of OSU's Benton Hall. It says: "Benjamin L. Arnold, a true friend, thorough teacher, and useful man."

Arnold was succeeded as college president by another Civil War veteran. The new president, John McKnight Bloss, was a Union man, a veteran of the 27th Indiana Volunteer Infantry who, like Arnold and Hawthorne, had been in the fight at Gettysburg. One of the new president's first acts was to change the uniform of the cadet corps from Arnold's favored gray to Union blue.

Rebel Yell in Eugene

After eleven years heading the Agriculture Department in Corvallis, Hawthorne became increasingly eager to teach classes of a more academic nature. The University of Oregon offered him the opportunity, and in 1884, he moved to Eugene to teach romance languages. The Board of Regents gave Hawthorne permission to spend his summers taking courses in psychology at Johns Hopkins University. After several summers of study, Hawthorne was confident enough in his abilities to establish a formal curriculum of psychology at Oregon. With $150 approved by the regents, Hawthorne outfitted a lab in the building that is now the University Club and, in 1895, founded the Department of Psychology at the University of Oregon.

Hawthorne retired from teaching in 1908 after a career that spanned more than forty years, during which he taught over thirty different courses. He found retirement boring, so at the age of seventy-four, Hawthorne enrolled in the U of O law school, from which he graduated in one year. He was admitted to the bar and practiced law in Eugene for years.

Hawthorne was a popular instructor at Oregon and a well-known and respected member of the Eugene community, although he had a reputation for being eccentric. He was an unrepentant Rebel who would show up in a full Confederate dress uniform at annual GAR parades and holler Rebel yells at the Union veterans as they marched down the streets of Eugene.

Benjamin J. Hawthorne lived until the age of ninety. He died on February 3, 1928, and is buried in the Eugene Masonic Cemetery south of the U of O campus. An impressive black granite monument marks Hawthorne's grave. His son Wistar Hawthorne, who died in the Spanish-American War, is buried next to him. President Benjamin Arnold is buried beneath a large white marble cross at Crystal Lake Cemetery in Corvallis, not far from the OSU campus. Neither man's monument mentions his service in the Civil War. Today, both men are best remembered for their contributions to higher education in the earliest years of the Oregon college system—but they were soldiers once.

The Minister and the General

Former Foes Reunited in Corvallis

The general passed away on a summer's day in Corvallis in 1915. The old soldier's end had come some fifty years and three thousand miles from where his gallantry had earned honor and promotion on the field of battle. A local minister with whom the general was well acquainted delivered his eulogy. Both the general and the minister were known and respected members of Corvallis, but the two men shared a common bond from a Virginia battlefield a half century earlier: the minister had once been the prisoner of the general.

The general was Thomas Jones Thorp, the handsome and dashing cavalry commander of the 1st New York Dragoons. The minister was the distinguished Reverend Dr. J.R.N. Bell of the Corvallis Presbyterian Church, regent of Oregon Agricultural College and former Confederate soldier.

THORP ANSWERS THE UNION CALL

Born to a prominent family in upstate New York, the grandson of Revolutionary War soldiers on both sides of his family, Thorp was a senior at Union College when the Civil War began. He left school to join the army and received his diploma while in the field. Thorp was appointed captain of the 85th New York Volunteer Infantry Regiment, where he distinguished himself as a company commander and was considered a master of drill and discipline. Wounded in the leg at the Battle of Fair Oaks in May 1862,

Thomas and Mandana Thorp were married in front of Thorp's regiment. *Courtesy of Allegany County, New York Historical Society.*

Thorp was sent home to recover from his injuries. While he was home, he was appointed by the governor as lieutenant colonel of a new regiment to be recruited from the state. During the summer of 1862, patriotic rallies were held throughout towns in Allegany and Livingston Counties to inspire volunteers to enlist in the new 130th New York Infantry. The regiment's officers, Colonel Alfred Gibbs and Lieutenant Colonel Thorp, would address the crowds, the band would play nationalistic tunes and the gathering would conclude with Miss Mandana Major, the accomplished and lovely nineteen-year-old daughter of Colonel John Major, singing "Rally 'round the Flag." Enough volunteers joined to form two regiments.

The 130th New York completed its training in September 1862. On the day the soldiers were to leave for the war, the entire command, 1,400 men strong, formed on the parade ground to witness the marriage of Lieutenant Colonel Thorp to Mandana Major. The ceremony was conducted within the hollow square formed by the regiment and presided over by the Reverend Joel Wakeman, a captain in the regiment. The newlyweds exited the service under an arch of crossed sabers.

The officers and men of the 130th New York distinguished themselves at the Siege of Suffolk. When the Union needed more cavalry troops, the foot soldiers were mounted and redesignated as the 1st Regiment, New York Dragoons. The Dragoons were assigned under the command of General Phil Sheridan. By the end of the war, the Dragoons had seen as much action and were as glorious in battle as any cavalry regiment in the Union army.

In June 1864, Thorp was wounded again and taken prisoner at the Battle of Trevellian Station. Confined to a prisoner of war camp in Georgia, Thorp celebrated the Fourth of July with a fiery and defiant speech to his fellow prisoners. His captors, fearing he would incite an uprising or lead an escape attempt, placed Thorp in isolation. They decided to transfer him to another POW camp and put him under guard on a train to Charleston. As the train steamed through the South Carolina night, the guards fell asleep, and Thorp escaped by leaping from the moving train into darkness. Evading recapture by hiding in the day and traveling only at night, living off the land and foraging for food, Thorp made his way through enemy territory and past Confederate pickets until he was able to rejoin his regiment near Richmond. For this feat of daring, Thorp was promoted to full colonel and given command of the Dragoons, replacing Colonel Gibbs, who had been promoted to brigadier general.

THEOLOGY STUDENT JOINS CONFEDERATES

John Richard Newton Bell was known throughout life simply by his initials, J.R.N. When the Civil War began, Bell was a theology student at tiny Wytheville College in southern Virginia, not too far from the border with North Carolina. In the nineteenth century, the curriculum of most southern schools included military instruction. Just sixteen years old in 1861, Bell and his fellow students were mustered into the Confederate army as the Wytheville Grays. Originally entered into service as a cavalry unit, the Grays were dismounted in 1863 and re-formed as Company I of the 26th Virginia Infantry Battalion. Fifty years later, Bell would recall in a newspaper interview that "lots of the boys were not much taller than their guns, but they were Virginians. They could fight." By Bell's account, he fought in thirty-two major battles and was bayoneted through the shoulder when his regiment fought with clubbed muskets against the Union charge at Cold Harbor. By the time he would face Thorp's Dragoons at the Battle of Cedar Creek, Private Bell was a seasoned veteran.

It was October 1864, and the Union army was raiding the Shenandoah Valley, burning crops and farms and killing livestock. Its mission was to destroy the Confederate economy and deprive the enemy of food and supplies. On October 18, the Federal soldiers stopped to rest and make camp in the beautiful autumn weather of the Virginia countryside, along pastoral Cedar Creek. Believing no hostile action was imminent, General Sheridan left his troops to confer with War Department officials in the town of Winchester, twenty miles away. The thirty thousand troops in blue were completely unaware that a Confederate army under Jubal Early was closing on their column. The Southerners had marched through the night and, at dawn, launched one of the most daring large-scale surprise attacks of the war. Bell's regiment of Virginians was assigned to attack the center of the Union line along the Valley Turnpike Road. Hundreds of Union prisoners were captured, many still in their underwear. Early's men had been on the march without food or sleep for twenty-four to thirty-six hours before the battle began, and as the Northern troops fled in panic, the exhausted and hungry Rebels halted to forage for food and other supplies from the abandoned tents and cooking fires. This break in the action allowed time for the Union troops to form a defensive line. Sheridan was alerted of the attack, and his mad dash to the battle has been immortalized in the poem "Sheridan's Ride" by Thomas Buchanan Read.

Sheridan rallied his cavalry brigades commanded by Wesley Merritt (whose second brigade included Thorp's Dragoons) and George Armstrong

Custer. At three o'clock in the afternoon, Merritt's horsemen counterattacked down the same Valley Turnpike Road that Bell had marched up that morning. Twice the Dragoons charged the Rebels, and each time they were compelled to retire under terrible fire. On the third attempt, the 6th New York Cavalry stormed the bridge over Cedar Creek, and the Dragoons swept down the road and crashed through a living wall of the enemy. The mounted counterattack broke the Confederate line and turned the tide of battle. What had looked to be a significant Confederate victory that morning had turned into a devastating defeat by sundown. With the defeat of Early's army, the Shenandoah Valley was left unprotected. Hundreds of Confederate soldiers were killed, with many more taken prisoners. Among the 352 prisoners captured by the New York Dragoons was J.R.N. Bell. Private Bell's battalion was nearly wiped out at Cedar Creek. Of the original 86 members of his company, only 4 men were still in service at the end of the war. Thorp continued on to fight more battles, but Bell was sent to a prisoner of war camp. Within six months, the Civil War was over and Bell returned home. He was nineteen years old and penniless.

The Veterans Head West

Upon his return to Virginia, Bell found work teaching school at the Oakwood Institute, which was eighty miles west of his hometown of Wytheville. Another instructor at the institute was Miss Margaret Kirk, whom Bell described as the "prettiest girl he had ever seen," and he told her so by hickory. Bell's first romantic kiss of his life was when he kissed his bride at his own wedding. The newlyweds returned to Wytheville, where Bell continued his studies while his wife taught school to pay his tuition. Upon graduation, Bell was ordained in the Methodist Episcopal Church South and assigned his first pastorate in Arkansas. The rough and rustic Arkansas life did not suit the couple used to the genteel society of Old Virginia, and in 1874, they headed west. By the time the couple arrived in Ashland, all the money they had in the world was a single silver dollar. Bell took work where he could find it. He cleared ditches, cut firewood and worked in the fields of southern Oregon—anything to pay for the groceries. He attended a local revival meeting and was ordained in the Southern Methodist Church and given charge of the church at Ashland. With that appointment, the Reverend J.R.N. Bell was called to the ministry in Oregon in a career that would span more than fifty years. His work would take him from Ashland to Corvallis, to Douglas County, to Independence, to Baker City, to California, back to Baker City and finally back to Corvallis in 1907. Ordained by both the Presbyterians and the Methodists, Bell was also grand chaplain of Masons longer than anyone else in U.S. history. He was known as the "marrying parson" because he presided at the weddings of more than one thousand couples, all of whose names he recorded in a thumb-worn notebook he kept with him. The children, and even grandchildren, of couples he had married would seek Bell out to perform their weddings. Bell was a guest preacher in hundreds of churches, regardless of denomination, and was the best-known clergyman in Oregon. While preaching in Douglas County, Bell purchased the *Roseburg Review*. In Independence, he published the *Independence West Side* and the *Monmouth Democrat*. He also founded the *Oregon School Journal*. In addition, Oregon governor Sylvester Pennoyer appointed Bell clerk of the State Railroad Commission.

Reverend J.R.N. Bell.
Courtesy OSU Archives.

Following the victory at Cedar Creek, Thorp led his men in battles throughout Virginia and was present at Appomattox when Lee surrendered to Grant. During the war, Thorp's Dragoons took part in more than sixty-five engagements and captured 1,533 prisoners, nineteen pieces of artillery and four Confederate battle flags. Not content to sit at home, Mandana Thorp joined her husband in the field, where she cared for the wounded and the sick in camp and in the hospital. At the end of the Civil War, at the ripe old age of twenty-eight, Thorp was promoted to brevet brigadier general of U.S. Volunteers. He proudly led his Dragoons in the Grand Review of the Union army through the streets of Washington along with 150,000 soldiers. The Grand Review took two days to pass in front of the White House, where President Johnson and General Grant reviewed the troops. Riding at General Thorp's side at the head of his regiment was his wife, Mandana.

The Civil War was hard on the Thorp family. Thomas was wounded five times. His younger brother, Captain Alexander Thorp, was killed at the Battle of Winchester. Another brother, Simeon Montgomery Thorp, a state senator in Kansas, was murdered when guerrillas under William Quantrill sacked the town of Lawrence. Like so many other combat veterans, Thomas and Mandana Thorp headed west to begin a new life. In the 1870s and 1880s, they lived and farmed in Michigan. In addition to farming, Thorp took up the study of mechanics and patented several devices he invented, including a type of metal fence post and wheel bearings for farm machinery. Leaving Michigan, the Thorps spent some time in Arizona Territory, where they engaged in the sheep and wool industry. Mrs. Thorp worked with her husband, often guarding the camp located in the valley of the Little Colorado River, adjacent to the reservation of the Navajo Indian Nation, while her husband was absent on business. The Thorps had five children, four daughters and a son. Sadly, as was common for the times, only the son and one daughter would live to adulthood. By 1893, Thorp was living in Forest Grove, where his two surviving children were enrolled at Pacific University.

General Thorp was in his sixties when he and his wife arrived in Corvallis about 1900. Through his membership in the Grand Army of the Republic, the fraternal organization of Civil War veterans, he became acquainted with the other former soldiers in the area. Mrs. Thorp was active as well, serving as president of the Women's Relief Corp and a leader of the Temperance movement. At some point, Thorp met Dr. Bell, and through their conversations and reminisces, the two old soldiers came to realize that they had faced each other on the field of battle. The dashing Yankee cavalry officer and the teenage theology student had become gray with age, yet they refought the Battle of Cedar Creek over and over again in words. While Thorp was proud of the title "General," Bell was equally as proud to have served as a private and often joked that he was the "only private Confederate soldier who survived the war. All the rest are colonels or majors, or captains." While the general and the minister had no knowledge of each other in 1864, they forged an enduring friendship fifty years later. In an era when the scars of the Civil War were real and continued to cause conflict throughout the United States, one old Virginian and an aged New Yorker found amity, admiration and mutual respect from common bonds.

A Different Kind of Civil War

In 1874, Bell became a member of the Board of Trustees of Oregon Agricultural College and later became a regent of the school. When intercollegiate athletics began, Bell was one of the program's most ardent supporters. He was among the spectators at the first football game between

Crowds watch as J.R.N. Bell tosses his hat into the Marys River following a Beaver Civil War football victory. *Courtesy OSU Archives.*

OAC and the University of Oregon. The rivalry between the two schools is the oldest college football rivalry on the West Coast. The annual game between the Oregon Ducks and Oregon State Beavers (formerly OAC) is universally known as the Civil War. In the excitement of the first OAC victory in 1894, Bell marched from the Corvallis campus to the nearby Marys River and threw his bowler hat into the water. A new tradition was born, and with each Civil War victory, Bell would repeat his march to the river and throw another hat into the water. The march grew into one of the most anticipated Corvallis social events of the year, and by the 1920s, thousands of football fans would make the victory walk to the river with him. Fundraisers were held to pay for his hats. In 1921, Oregon State named the football stadium in his honor, and Bell Field was the home of the Beavers until 1953.

Dr. Bell passed away in 1928, and his wife, Margaret, died in 1939. They are buried in Crystal Lake Cemetery, not too far from the Marys River where he threw his hats. The couple shares a large granite monument, which includes the square and compass of the Masons above their names.

THORP GRAVE LACKS HEADSTONE

The death of General Thorp was front-page news in the *Daily Gazette Times*. His funeral was held at Bell's Presbyterian Church, and he was laid to rest in a plot owned by the GAR in Crystal Lake Cemetery. Following her husband's death, Mrs. Thorp moved to Portland to be near her daughter. Thorp was so highly respected that the U.S. Congress passed a bill to provide his widow a pension of thirty dollars a month, yet for some unknown reason, Thorp's grave was not marked. The grave would remain unmarked for ninety-two years, until it came to the attention of local members of the Sons of Union Veterans of the Civil War (SUVCW). With the help of Judy Juntunen, a cemetery volunteer, Thorp's final resting place was identified. A proper military headstone was provided by the Department of Veterans Affairs, and on a sunny Saturday in February 2008, members of the SUVCW installed the white marble monument on Thorp's grave. The general rests peacefully under a large oak tree, not too far from the grave of his old friend the minister.

A Forgotten Hero

A Medal of Honor Grave Goes Unmarked

Roy Vanderhoof enjoys taking pictures. Driving his car down Portland's meandering Terwilliger Boulevard, he planned to photograph the grave of Hartwell Compson at the Grand Army of the Republic Cemetery. Vanderhoof had come across a website that listed the burial sites of Medal of Honor recipients. While photographs of graves in other states had been posted to the website, few of the final resting places of the fifteen Medal of Honor winners buried in Oregon were pictured. Compson, a Union cavalry officer who had received the Medal of Honor in the Civil War, was among the graves without pictures. Vanderhoof decided he would be the person to record the visual history of the graves of these American heroes.

Vanderhoof thought photographing the grave would be simple because Compson was buried just a few miles from his Portland home. As it turned out, the cemetery itself was not easy to find. Located on Boones Ferry Road, the two-acre GAR Cemetery is adjacent to a much larger graveyard— Greenwood Hills Cemetery. Although the GAR Cemetery is a separate entity, it is not marked from the road, and you must turn in to Greenwood Hills to find it. Once he found the place, Vanderhoof parked his car and headed down the hill to find Compson's grave, which is located in Section 4, plot 136A. He found the section marker underneath a tree, but where the headstone should have been was an empty patch of ground. He rechecked the plot number and searched the surrounding area. Nothing! Incredibly, an American war hero was buried in an unmarked grave. Vanderhoof stared in disbelief at the barren piece of Oregon earth.

COMPSON IN THE CIVIL WAR

One hundred and forty years earlier, a young Hartwell Compson stared in disbelief himself. In the heat of battle, through the smoke and stench and sound of gunfire, a colorful movement caught his eye. Compson was a Union army officer, a lieutenant colonel in command of the 8th New York Cavalry Regiment. Compson, the second of thirteen children born to Jonas and Ruth Compson, was raised on his parents' farm near Tyre, New York. Compson was nineteen when he joined the cavalry as a private. Proving himself a talented and respected soldier, he rose swiftly through the ranks, advancing to corporal and then sergeant. He was commissioned a second lieutenant on April 15, 1863, and promoted to first lieutenant four months later. In March 1864, Compson was promoted to captain and placed in command of a cavalry troop. Appointed major in December 1864, he was made commander of the 8th New York Cavalry and brevetted to lieutenant colonel

of U.S. Volunteers on February 28, 1865. By the end of the war, the valiant Compson had fought in forty-five major engagements, including Fredericksburg, Gettysburg and Cold Harbor. He was wounded twice and had two horses shot from beneath him. A week after assuming command of the 8th, Compson found himself facing Confederate forces outside Waynesboro, Virginia. A seasoned veteran at twenty-two years of age, Compson was the youngest regimental commander in a cavalry division commanded by the boy general: George Armstrong Custer.

At Waynesboro, Custer split his cavalry brigades into two forces. At two o'clock in the afternoon, Custer ordered three of his regiments, each man armed with a Spencer repeating rifle, to dismount and attack the

The Philadelphia mint designed the original Medal of Honor, which remained unchanged until 1895. *Courtesy of the Congressional Medal of Honor Society.*

enemy flank from a heavily wooded area. In a simultaneous assault, Union artillery opened fire and Custer's mounted regiments, including Compson's New Yorkers, charged the opposite flank and crashed through to the center of the battle line. Compson led his Yankee horse cavalry past Rebel cannon, where his men fought hand to hand with Confederate infantry. The clash of cold steel filled Compson's ears as sword struck bayonet and musket. It was at that point that movement and color caught Compson's eye, causing him to stare, at least momentarily, in amazement.

What Compson had spotted was the red and white flag of a Confederate Army Headquarters. The enemy commander, General Jubal Early, was leading his staff to the front to personally direct the battle. Compson did not hesitate: with a bugler at one side and a flag-bearer the other, the colonel spurred his horse and led a charge directly at the Southern officers. Compson zeroed in on the enemy flag. Seizing the flagstaff with one hand, Compson swung the back of his heavy cavalry saber at the enemy color-bearer, who refused to relinquish his banner. Suddenly, the battle between four thousand soldiers was reduced to two men: close, personal, desperate and bloody. A final blow from Compson's sword unhorsed the brave opponent, who was never to rise again, and Compson held the enemy colors. In the meantime,

This flag, captured by Compson, was returned to Virginia in 1906. The flag measures four by six feet. *Courtesy of the Museum of the Confederacy, Richmond, Virginia. Photo by Katherine Wetzel.*

the Confederate senior officers had scattered in disarray. The Union rout was on!

Compson handed the flag to one of his men and dashed after the Rebels. Early had escaped across a bridge, but some of his senior aides were captured. By the end of the day, Compson's regiment alone had taken eight hundred prisoners, five pieces of artillery, 1,500 stands of small arms and eight enemy battle flags. Other Federal regiments captured an additional nine flags.

Twenty-first-century Americans often fail to understand the significance of military flags in the nineteenth century. Not only were the flags symbols of pride and great honor, but they also held strategic importance. A commander could identify the location of individual regiments on the battlefield by locating their large standards. The headquarters flag that Compson captured signaled the presence of the commanding general on the field of conflict—a presence meant to rally men to victory. Although Early had escaped the fate of his flag, Waynesboro would be his last major battle. His army had been destroyed.

When General Sheridan arrived after the battle, the twenty-five-year-old Custer greeted his boss with a display typical of the general's flamboyance. Each of the seventeen captured Rebel flags was paraded, streaming in the wind, by a Union cavalryman. It was a great spectacle and the sort of thing Custer thoroughly enjoyed. That evening, Compson was summoned to Sheridan's headquarters, where he received the personal compliments of the general and a battlefield promotion to full colonel.

Compson was assigned to carry Sheridan's dispatches to Washington and to personally deliver the captured flags to the secretary of war. While in Washington, Brevet Colonel Thomas Hartwell Benton Compson was awarded the Congressional Medal of Honor for the capture of General Early's headquarters flag at the Battle of Waynesboro. Unlike many veterans whose heroics were not recognized until decades after the Civil War, Compson received his medal less than thirty days after the battle. In addition to the medal, Compson was granted a thirty-day leave and free transportation to any part of the country he cared to travel to. Compson used his time off to visit his wife, Mary, in western New York State.

By the time Compson returned to his regiment, Lee had surrendered to Grant. Union victory brought an end to this stage of Compson's military career. He rode at the head of his 8th New York Cavalry in the Grand Review of the Union army in Washington. He mustered out of the army with his regiment on June 27, 1865. The hero was once again a civilian.

GO WEST, YOUNG MAN

Peace sent Compson back to his New York home, where Hartwell and Mary soon had a baby girl. The adventures and tribulations of the war had made Compson restless, and he was soon heading west. By 1870, he was living in Grand Rapids, Michigan, where he made his living as a carpenter. In 1880, Compson was trying his luck in the silver mines of Frisco, Utah, while his wife and daughter lived in Chicago. The Compsons eventually divorced, and Mary returned to New York.

Moving often and trying his hand at many trades, Compson served stints as a U.S. marshal and postmaster and worked as a farmer. By 1887, he was teaching on the Klamath Indian Reservation in southern Oregon. It was in Oregon that Compson again rose to prominence. His war record earned him an appointment as brigadier general of the Oregon National Guard and president of the State Military Board. Compson would be addressed as general for the rest of his life. Leaving Klamath Falls, General Compson relocated to Portland, where he worked as a real estate broker and kept a home at 186 Morrison Street. He developed an active interest in Oregon politics and was mentioned as a possible candidate for governor. The GAR named its St. Johns post in his honor.

It took ninety-nine years for Compson's grave to receive a headstone. *Photo by Karen Fletcher.*

The general died in Portland on August 31, 1905. He was sixty-three years old. Compson was laid to rest with his Civil War comrades at the Grand Army of the Republic Cemetery. Records indicate that a monument was planned for his grave, but it was never erected. Time passed, and Compson's burial plot remained unmarked as his memory faded and a century passed.

After discovering Compson's grave unmarked, Roy Vanderhoof sprung into action. He contacted the Department of Veterans Affairs, which provided a headstone, and on a fall Saturday, ninety-nine years after the general's death, more than two hundred people attended the dedication of a new headstone for Hartwell Compson, an American hero no longer forgotten.

From Plantation to Pulpit

Former Slave Becomes Portland Minister

In the motion picture *Glory*, black Union soldiers march into a Southern town as amazed slave children gather to watch them. Sergeant Rawlins, portrayed by Morgan Freeman, says to the children, "Ain't no dream. We runaway slaves, but we come back fightin' men. Go tell your folks how kingdom come in the year of jubilee!" The character played by Freeman is incredibly similar to the life of a Portland man. Daniel Drew was born a slave but died a free man. He fought for his liberty because freedom is never given and must be earned. He took up the musket, donned the blue suit and persevered against those who would keep him enslaved.

Little is known of Drew's early life. He was born in Virginia about 1843. His grandparents were Africans, taken prisoner in their native land and shipped in chains to the Americas. We don't know the name of the white man who owned Drew; census records do not list slaves by name. They are listed by sex and age on a special census schedule just like head of cattle or bushels of wheat. We do know that the outbreak of the Civil War found young Daniel laboring in Arkansas. He was twenty years old the day the Union army arrived at his master's farm.

For the first time in his life, Drew was free to travel without a pass. He made his way to St. Louis, where the army was recruiting free black men to fight the Southern rebellion. Drew signed up as a private in the 3rd Arkansas Infantry (African Descent). The 3rd was sent to Helena, Arkansas, where it was used for garrison and guard duty. After six months, the regiment was reorganized and redesignated as the 56th U.S. Colored Infantry. Their commanding officer was Colonel Carl Bentzoni, a tough Prussian who trained his men for combat duty. Their chance to fight came in the summer of 1864, when 360 men from the U.S. Colored Infantry and a battery from the 2nd Colored Artillery were ordered to march to Wallace's Ferry. Their orders were to seek and destroy enemy cavalry that was raiding farms in Union-occupied territory.

BAPTIZED IN BATTLE

On a hot and dusty Tuesday dawn, the Federal forces were attacked by one thousand Arkansas and Missouri cavalrymen under Colonel Archibald Dobbins. Taken by surprise, the Union cannon crews were shot down before they could fire the big guns, and all the white officers were killed or wounded. The black infantrymen formed a battle line and for the next four hours fought desperately, free men standing shoulder to shoulder in a fight for their lives, the barrels of their muskets getting so hot they would burn flesh.

Confederate colonel Archibald Dobbins. *Library of Congress.*

At about ten o'clock that morning, the black foot soldiers were joined by 150 mounted men of the 15th Illinois Cavalry who had raced in with drawn sabers and sliced their way through a portion of Dobbins's horsemen. The combined force, black infantry and white cavalry, began a fighting retreat back to its fort at Helena. Under constant assault from all sides, the black troops made a countercharge into the Rebel line. Their gallant thrust broke the gray cavalry and drove away the pursuit. The Federal forces made it back to their post without further attack. Union casualties were 4 officers and 21 enlisted men killed or mortally wounded.

Private Drew and his comrades had proven their bravery on the field of battle, and for the rest of 1864 through the end of the war, they would fight engagements throughout Arkansas and parts of Mississippi. As black soldiers proved themselves in battle throughout the Civil War, abolitionist Frederick Douglass began advocating for full citizenship. In an 1863 speech in Philadelphia, Douglass said, "Once let the black man get upon his person the brass letter, U.S., let him get an eagle on his button, and a musket on his shoulder and bullets in his pocket, there is no power on earth that can deny that he has earned the right to citizenship."

With the fall of the Confederacy, Drew and the men of the 56th peacefully performed garrison duty at Helena until their enlistments were complete. The end of their service would bring a tragedy many times deadlier than battle. The men of the 56th, having completed their enlistment, were loaded on two steam ships that were to transport them from Helena to St. Louis, where they would be paid and discharged from the army. As the ships made their way up the Mississippi, several of the men took ill and died. The ships arrived at St. Louis at night, and the troops were kept on board until morning, when doctors came on board. The diagnosis was cholera, and Drew and the men were ordered to a quarantine station.

Cholera is an intestinal disease marked by exhaustive diarrhea and sudden drops in blood pressure. In its most severe form, cholera is one of the fastest killers known to man. Death often occurs within a few hours. The men of the 56th, proud, free and victorious in battle, were defeated by disease. A full-strength infantry regiment numbered 1,000 soldiers. Over a three-week period in 1866, the 56th regiment lost 649 men to a microscopic killer. The dead were buried together in the Jefferson Barracks National Cemetery in St. Louis. Daniel Drew was among fewer than 300 survivors.

Civilian Life

After the epidemic had passed, the surviving soldiers were processed for discharge. Most of the men had nowhere to go and owned no possessions beyond their military uniforms. Once paid, the first order of business for the men was to buy civilian clothes. Although emancipated and flush with

Ex-slave Daniel Drew became chaplain of the Oregon GAR. *Author's collection.*

army greenbacks, the black troopers were not welcome in St. Louis shops. Instead, the haberdashers sent runners to the barracks with samples of material, and they took measurements and orders from the soldiers. Tailors in town would make the clothing, and the runners would deliver the packages to the barracks. Black wool suits were the most popular item purchased.

Daniel Drew, a free man in a new suit, left the army and began a new life. He headed back to his old army post in Helena, where, during the war, Quakers under protection of the army had founded a school for black people near the fort. Colonel Bentzoni and men of the 56th donated funds from their pay to purchase thirty acres for the school, which was named the Southland Institute. Drew became one of the school's first fifteen students.

In 1871, Drew was ordained a minister by the Society of Friends, and he became a well-known evangelist in the Helena area. He took a wife and started a family. To supplement his preaching income, Drew and his wife, Laura Ann, operated a farm in Cleburne, Arkansas.

After the turn of the twentieth century, Daniel and Laura Ann moved to Portland, accompanied by son William and his family. They joined the Sunnyside Quaker's Meeting, but in 1907, Drew became a minister in the African Methodist Episcopal Church.

MEMBERSHIP IN THE GAR

In Oregon, Reverend Drew became active in the Grand Army of the Republic. At a time when most of America was segregated, the GAR was integrated and welcomed black Union veterans into the organization. Drew joined Portland's Benjamin Butler Post 57.

One of the projects of the GAR was to raise money for a soldiers' memorial at Portland's Lone Fir Cemetery. Drew was one of the fundraisers for the monument. The November 17, 1902 edition of the *Oregonian* carried a notice for a lecture by Reverend Daniel Drew, an ex-slave, who would be speaking on "The Condition of the Colored Race Before, During, and Since the Civil War." The lecture was held at the Sunnyside Congregational Church and was a benefit for the Lone Fir Monument Association. The newspaper declared that the lecture program would include patriotic music and southern melodies by the Congregational church choir. The fundraising was successful, and the soldiers' monument was erected at Lone Fir at a cost of $3,500.

For the remainder of his life, Drew remained active in the GAR. In 1919, at the GAR encampment held at the Dalles, Reverend Drew was elected chaplain of the Department of Oregon—a remarkable achievement for one of just a handful of black Civil War veterans who lived in Oregon.

Daniel and Laura Drew lived out their life in their home at 1759 Courtenay Street in North Portland. The 1920 census recorded that he worked as a

Daniel Drew's name appears on plaque C-68 of the African American Civil War Memorial in Washington, D.C. *Photo by author.*

laborer in the local gardens. Reverend Daniel W. Drew passed away on March 10, 1923, and was laid to rest in Portland's historic Columbian Cemetery. A simple soldier's headstone marks the final resting place of a man who led a most remarkable life best summarized by Drew's own words, which closed his chaplain's report to the GAR: "Let us be at our best at all times, supporting and encouraging in every possible way those things that are just and right that we may have the approval of the great Judge when we shall be called before Him."

NOTE: Oregon did not always welcome African Americans (exclusion laws were on the books until 1926). This fact makes Drew's achievements even more impressive. Nearly 200,000 free men of color served in the Union army, but there are just 13 African American Civil War veterans known to be buried in Oregon.

NAME	REGIMENT	CEMETERY
Cpl. Samuel A. Arbuckle	29th U.S. Colored Infantry	GAR Cemetery—Portland
Pvt. Manuel E. Corbin	U.S. Colored Infantry	GAR Cemetery—Portland
Pvt. Daniel Drew	56th U.S. Colored Infantry	Columbian Cemetery—Portland
Tmstr. Hiram Gorman	Battle of Wilson's Creek	Salem Pioneer Cemetery
Sgt. Maj. John W. Jackson	U.S. Colored Infantry	Hayesville Cemetery—Salem
Pvt. Gilbert Jones	109th U.S. Colored Infantry	Unknown—Died Pendleton 1922
Sgt. Maj. Oliver W. Jones	65th U.S. Colored Infantry	Roseburg Veterans Cemetery
Bugler Daniel Shafer	102nd U.S. Colored Infantry	City View—Salem
Pvt. Charles A. Thomas	5th U.S. Col. Heavy Artillery	GAR Cemetery—Portland
Pvt. William H. Tuttle	U.S. Colored Infantry	Lone Fir—Portland
Pvt. Henry Willis	U.S. Colored Infantry	Lone Fir—Portland
Pvt. James Wisher	45th U.S. Colored Infantry	Linkville Pioneer—Klamath Falls
Cpl. Israel Woods	119th U.S. Colored Infantry	City View—Salem

Oregon's Confederate Engineer

Father of Portland's Water System

Turn on the water faucet in any kitchen in Portland and you will get a seemingly endless supply of safe, clean, clear, cold mountain water. It has pretty much been that way since 1895, when the pipeline from Bull Run Reservoir to Portland was designed and built by one of Robert E. Lee's best engineers. Isaac Smith is known as the father of Portland's water system, but he had an international career that made him one of the most significant civil engineers of the nineteenth century.

The son of a minister, Smith was born in Fredericksburg, Virginia, in 1826. He had a classic education, first at Fairfax College and then at Virginia Military Institute, from which he graduated in 1846. Hired as an assistant surveyor by the U.S. Army Engineers, he was dispatched to Maine, where he participated in marking and settling a dispute regarding the international border between the United States and Canada. His next assignment took him to our southern border, where he was commissioned as an officer during the Mexican War.

As a lieutenant in a light infantry regiment, Smith took part in the siege of Veracruz. After the war, Smith returned to civilian surveying in the employment of the federal government. Over the next five years, he established the boundaries between the Creek and Cherokee nations and the states of Iowa and Minnesota. His first trip to the Pacific Northwest came in 1855, when he was dispatched to survey and build lighthouses along the coast.

While working in Washington Territory, Smith met Governor Isaac Stevens, a West Point graduate and former army engineer who had also served at the siege of Veracruz. The two Isaacs formed a friendship based on their common experiences as military school cadets, professional engineers and war veterans. When Governor Stevens led the state militia in the

Portland women enjoy a drink of clean water thanks to Oregon's Confederate engineer. *Oregon Historical Society #bb006993.*

Yakima Indian Wars, Smith served as his aide-de-camp. At the close of the Indian campaign, Smith was appointed deputy surveyor for Washington, and Stevens became the territory's first delegate to Congress.

For the next four years, Smith held a series of government engineering jobs in Washington. At the outbreak of the Civil War, he was working as registrar of the land office in Olympia. Initially remaining in his job, Smith could no longer stay neutral when Federal troops invaded his native Virginia. Crossing the border into Canada, Smith worked in the gold fields to raise money for his steamship passage to Baltimore. Offering his services to the Confederate States of America, Smith was appointed captain of engineers. Shortly after reporting for duty, Smith learned that his friend from the Washington frontier, Isaac Stevens, had been appointed major general in the Union army and killed at the Battle of Chantilly.

Fort Stevens on the Oregon coast is named in honor of General Isaac Stevens. *Library of Congress.*

Captain Isaac Smith was sent to Richmond and placed in charge of the pontoon service. Smith's engineers would build bridges for Lee's army to advance across the Potomac River and then burn those same pontoon bridges after Lee's men would retreat back across the river. By 1864, Smith had risen to the rank of colonel and was instrumental in constructing the Confederate fortifications at Petersburg. Drawing on experience gained at the siege of Veracruz, Smith's engineers built an elaborate maze of earthworks and rifle pits. Siege combat was a preview of the murderous trench warfare that would take place in Europe fifty years later. The outnumbered and outgunned Rebels held out against Grant's repeated assaults for nine months. Finally, on April 2, 1865, Petersburg fell to a massive Union attack. Seven days later, Colonel Smith and the Confederate engineers surrendered at Appomattox with the rest of the Army of Northern Virginia.

After the surrender, Smith was broke. He returned to his father's home with nothing more than an old gray uniform, much tattered and worn, a good horse and a large amount of experience. With the United States unwilling to give top government jobs to ex-Confederates, Smith sailed for Mexico to continue his engineering career. Back in Veracruz twenty years after he had been part of a conquering army, Smith became district engineer on the Mexican Imperial Railroad. After three years south of the border, Smith was hired by Northern Pacific Railroad to conduct surveys in California, Oregon and Washington.

In 1872, Smith was in Oregon City, where he built the canals and locks around Willamette Falls. In 1874, he platted the city of Tacoma for the western terminus of the Northern Pacific Railroad. After Tacoma, Smith worked for the Canadian government, studying the feasibility of steamship travel along the Frasier River, and then went to Peru to work on the Trans-Andean Railroad. He then spent four years working for the State of California. He returned to Oregon and Washington in the employment of Northern Pacific.

In 1885, the City of Portland hired Smith as its first chief engineer and superintendent of the Water Committee. He was paid the princely salary of $400 per month. For the next decade, Colonel Smith, as he was called, developed the infrastructure for the growth of modern-day Portland. His first task was to find a route and construct a pipeline and reservoir from the Bull Run watershed to the Rose City. Oregon's Bull Run River shares the name of the Virginia creek where the first major battle of the Civil War took place but is not named after it. For several months, the survey party fought through country described by another member of the survey team as "rugged wilderness, unsurveyed and unknown. The only trails are those of elk, deer, etc. There is not a trace of civilization in any direction."

Other projects that Smith led included overseeing twenty-four miles of pipeline construction through old-growth forest and brush; planning and building headworks and the roads and bridges needed for the pipeline passage; overseeing upgrades of the city's mains and distribution pipe; and coordinating the construction of reservoirs at Mount Tabor and

Isaac W. Smith is known as the father of Portland's water system. *Courtesy of SCV Camp 458.*

Washington Park. Because of his dedicated service, Smith is known as the "father of Portland's water system."

In the cold and damp Portland winter of 1896, the great engineer contracted pneumonia. Colonel Isaac William Smith died on New Year's Day 1897. A lifelong bachelor, Smith's dedication to his work was legendary. His last words were "How is the wing dam in the Sandy getting along?" Smith was laid to rest in River View Cemetery. A simple headstone marks his grave.

In 1903, descendants of Confederate Civil War veterans living in Portland named their organization after Smith. Isaac W. Smith Camp 458 of the Sons of Confederate Veterans is still in existence today. The next time you quench your thirst with Portland water, give a nod to the old Civil War veteran who delivered it to you.

A Forlorn Hope

Vicksburg Charge Earns Medal of Honor

Ulysses S. Grant sent out the call for volunteers. He had spent months encircling the enemy, and now he had them trapped within their fortress on the Mississippi River. He would take that fort by storm, and this time, by God, he would not fail. Two days earlier, his men had been pushed back, but that assault had been hurried and made without careful planning and proper support. Grant had lost one thousand men in that attack. This time would be different: the Confederate stronghold at Vicksburg would fall.

Grant chose his best general, William Tecumseh Sherman, to lead the attack, which would be preceded by a bombardment from Union gunboats on the river. Vicksburg sat high on the bluffs of the Mississippi, protected on one side by the river and on the land side by steep cliffs and fortifications. In order to breach the fort, the Union troops would first have to cross a dry moat and then scale the heights in a direct strike. A volunteer storming party would lead Sherman's attack, with 150 carrying logs, planks and ladders. The plan was that some of the men would charge and throw the logs across the deep but dry moat while the men with planks would place them between the logs, creating bridges over the trench. This would allow the third group of volunteers to cross the moat with scaling ladders and place them against the enemy embankment. The main body of armed troops could then advance and attack the fort directly.

The mission would be a "forlorn hope," a nineteenth-century military term for a charge where most members could expect to be killed or wounded. Such an attack today would be called a suicide mission. Each regiment would have a quota for volunteers, and Sherman specified that only single men would be accepted—no fathers or husbands would be sent on this mission. Even with that limitation, twice as many men as needed stepped forward, and the volunteers were pared to the 150 required.

One of the volunteers was twenty-one-year-old Louis Renninger, who would one day make his home in Oregon. Renninger, the son of German immigrants, was born on his parents' farm in Liverpool, Ohio. He volunteered for the Union at the start of the war and was assigned to the 37th Ohio Volunteer Infantry, one of three all-German regiments from Ohio. The commander of the 37th was Colonel Edward Siber, a veteran of the Prussian army well known for discipline.

The naval bombardment of Vicksburg began at dawn on May 22, 1863. At the same time, Union artillery opened fire from their positions on land. Renninger could literally feel the earth shake as he waited for his part of the attack to begin. The big navy guns fell silent at ten o'clock that morning. It was time for the army to begin the assault.

Sherman ordered the volunteer storming party to move out. He would follow them with his entire army corps composed of nearly sixteen thousand Federal soldiers. Renninger was a seasoned veteran whose performance had earned him a promotion to corporal. His regiment had been engaged in combat operations for two years, but this mission was different. The volunteers had all faced the possibility of death or injury before; today, death or injury was a near certainty. Few men were expected to survive a forlorn hope.

The path of Sherman's attack was down the chillingly named Graveyard Road. Two of Grant's other corps would coordinate their assaults simultaneously with Sherman's men. The volunteers were initially protected from enemy fire by a ravine, but as they emerged from the chasm, they faced four hundred yards of open ground between themselves and the Confederate fortifications. The first party, groups of two men carrying logs, started at a dead run, but half of them were shot down. The next two groups, with the planks and scaling ladders, followed under withering fire, yet many reached the moat where the survivors of the first group had taken refuge.

One of the volunteers who was carrying planks, William Bumgarner of the 4th West Virginia, reported that fifteen bullets pierced the board he carried during the charge. The volunteers found it impossible to build bridges because so many of the logs had been dropped along the way. Exposed to deadly enemy musket fire and unwilling to retreat, the survivors sought shelter by diving into the ditch they had aimed to cross. Protected from direct musket fire, the men in the moat were still subject to attack.

William Tecumseh Sherman. *Library of Congress.*

The Confederate defenders would light the fuses on small bombs and toss or roll the primitive hand grenades into the moat, where they exploded. Occasionally, a Union soldier would grab the bomb while its fuse was still burning and throw it back at the Rebels. Sherman's main body of troops repeatedly pressed the attack forward, but each time, they were driven back, unable to breach the Rebel fortifications. Grant's other corps fared no better than Sherman.

Of the 150 volunteers, 72 were killed and most of the remainder were wounded. Sunset occurred at eight o'clock in the evening, and finally, after nearly ten hours hiding in the moat facing nonstop enemy musket fire and bombs, Louis Renninger and the survivors of the forlorn hope were able to retreat back to Union lines under the cover of darkness. The survivors who could walk carried or dragged those volunteers who were too badly wounded to retreat on their own. Renninger himself was bloodied; military records indicate that he was wounded in the shoulder and suffered an injury to his eye.

The forlorn hope was one of the most thrilling and tragic charges of the Civil War, but it proved to be a foolhardy undertaking. Grant lost 3,200 soldiers that day, while Confederate losses were fewer than 500 men. With the second straight failure of a frontal assault, Grant changed tactics and laid siege to Vicksburg. After seven weeks of constant bombardment, with little ammunition remaining and with his men and the civilian population facing starvation, Confederate general John Pemberton struck his colors and surrendered the city on July 4, 1863. The Union would take 30,000 prisoners and establish total control over the vital Mississippi River. The citizens of Vicksburg refused to celebrate the Fourth of July for the next eighty years.

RENNINGER HEADS TO OREGON

As a result of his injuries, Louis Renninger was transferred to the Veterans Reserve Corps, a branch of the army where disabled soldiers performed light duty while recovering from their wounds. Corporal Renninger completed his military service and was discharged on October 14, 1864. During the war, his regiment lost 206 enlisted men and officers killed or mortally wounded or dead from disease. Their losses at Vicksburg were 19 killed and 75 wounded; 20 percent of the stalwart German lads who had marched out of Ohio with Renninger never came home.

Upon returning to his Ohio farm, Renninger married German-born Elizabeth Mann, and they started a family that would grow to four sons and five daughters. About 1870, Louis and Elizabeth left Ohio for Michigan, where they bought a place near the tiny hamlet of Leavitt. They would farm their land for more than twenty years until harsh winters and the cold winds from Lake Michigan prompted them to seek the moderate climate of the Willamette Valley. By 1898, the Renningers had established a farm in the Marcola District of Lane County, east of Springfield. Once established in the area, Renninger, like many other Civil War veterans, joined the Grand Army of the Republic.

MEDAL OF HONOR

In the decades after the end of the Civil War, historians began to closely examine the battles of the war and the men who had fought them. In addition, the U.S. Army and the various states compiled histories of their regiments that had served in the conflict. Veterans groups such as the GAR examined individual acts of heroism, and congressional committees held hearings to scrutinize acts of valor. As a result, from 1890 to 1899, more Medals of Honor were awarded for Civil War action than were awarded during the war—a total of 683 Medals of Honor in the last decade of the nineteenth century. The events that occurred in Vicksburg had been overshadowed during their time by the Battle of Gettysburg. The military's review of the actions at Vicksburg resulted in the award of 127 Medals of Honor. The events of May 22, 1863, alone accounted for 96 of the medals, the highest one-day total in the medal's entire history. Seventy-eight still-living survivors of the forlorn hope were decorated with the Medal of Honor. Their citation reads simply: "Gallantry in the charge of the volunteer storming party." Corporal Louis Renninger of Company H, 37th Regiment Ohio Volunteer Infantry, was awarded his Medal of Honor on August 15, 1894.

On November 17, 1908, Louis Renninger left home for the last time. He had gone to his son's farm just a half mile away. When he did not return as expected, the family became alarmed and discovered Renninger's body in his son's barn. The local justice of the peace concluded he had died of a massive heart attack. Renninger was sixty-seven years old. He was

Medal of Honor plaque on Renninger's grave at Eugene Pioneer Cemetery. *Photo by author.*

laid to rest in the Eugene Pioneer Cemetery. The J.W. Geary Post of the GAR presided at the funeral, which was also attended by the Women's Relief Corps and the Ladies of the GAR, along with Renninger's family and many friends.

The *Eugene Daily Guard* reported the death and covered the funeral, yet the newspaper made no mention of the Medal of Honor. When they died years later, Renninger's wife Elizabeth and daughter Maude were buried next to him in the family plot. In 2008, one hundred years after Louis Renninger's death, the Sons of Union Veterans of the Civil War named a new camp in Springfield in his honor.

Storming the Ramparts

Oregonians Display Courage in North Carolina

The final assault would come from land and sea. Aboard the USS *Gettysburg*, navy lieutenant Roswell Lamson of Willamina, Oregon, prepared to storm the beach. Lamson dressed in his finest uniform. His long blue frock coat with a double row of gleaming buttons was completed with sash, sword and pistol. He would lead an assault force of U.S. sailors and marines against the Confederate stronghold Fort Fisher. The *Gettysburg* and fifty-five more Union ships of the line had been bombarding the fort for two earth-shattering days. The fleet's guns were about to fall silent.

On land, despite the winter chill, beads of sweat formed on the brow of seventeen-year-old soldier Alaric Chapin. He could not hear the navy guns over the roar of army artillery to his rear. The teenager, one of thirteen volunteers armed with axes, would be the spear point of the coordinated land assault against the fort. It was a little past midday on January 15, 1865. The assault would begin in two hours.

Fort Fisher, built from earth and sand, with walls as high as thirty feet, was ideal to absorb enemy shelling. Protected by forty-seven heavy guns, the fort guarded the mouth of the Cape Fear River, twenty-nine miles upstream from Wilmington, North Carolina. The Rebel garrison force numbered about 2,000 men under the command of Colonel William Lamb. On a peninsula just north of the fort were positioned another 6,400 hundred soldiers. The fort, called the Gibraltar of the South, protected Robert E. Lee's last major supply route to Virginia. The Union had previously tried and failed to take Fort Fisher in December.

As time for the attack neared, Lamson boarded a small boat with his men, who began rowing for the sandy beach. Lamson, twenty-six years old, was the captain of the *Gettysburg*. Although he was born in Iowa, Lamson's boyhood reads like a history of Oregon. He was nine years old when he crossed the Oregon Trail with his parents, who took a Donation Land Claim near Willamina. Young Roswell was sent to the Oregon Institute at Salem for his education. After school, he joined the militia, fought in the Yakima Indian War and was present at the large battle that took place near where La Grande is now located. In 1858, Lamson became the first Oregonian appointed to the U.S. Naval Academy. On his journey from Oregon to Annapolis, Lamson stopped at the Ohio home of his uncle, General C.P. Buckingham. The general's beautiful young daughter Catherine, whom everyone called Kate, was just fifteen at the time. Kate began a correspondence with her older cousin Roswell that would continue throughout the war and beyond.

Lamson proved to be an outstanding midshipman. He was in his senior year at Annapolis when the Civil War began, and he took his final exams at sea, graduating second in the class of 1862. Lamson rose quickly in the ranks and was soon given command of the Union gunboat USS *Mount Washington*.

Roswell Lamson from Willamina was the first Oregon cadet at the U.S. Naval Academy. *Naval Historical Society.*

While supporting army operations along the James River in 1863, Lamson and the *Mount Washington* engaged in a fierce battle with Confederate artillery and infantry. The ship's boiler was destroyed, and the powerless and grounded *Mount Washington* had to repel boarders before being rescued and towed to safety by another gunboat. The *Mount Washington* lost five men dead and fourteen wounded. Lamson's courage and steady leadership under fire in this engagement were cited in dispatches from the secretary of the navy. To be mentioned in dispatches is a great honor for military personnel.

Oregon newspapers covered Lamson's heroics, which had his father speculating on financial opportunities that waited after the war. The elder Lamson wrote to his son, "The people of Oregon feel proud." Roswell Lamson went on to command more ships and flotillas than any other officer of his rank or age in the Civil War, climaxed by his captaincy of the navy's fastest ship, the USS *Gettysburg*.

The *Gettysburg* was a 950-ton steam-powered ship of the line, 221 feet in length with seven guns and a crew of ninety-six officers and men. With a top speed of fifteen knots, the *Gettysburg* was swift on the water and captured seven Rebel blockade runners; their prize money was shared by Lamson and his crew. Prize money, a powerful incentive for Union sailors, was awarded by the Navy Department based on the value of the captured ship and its cargo. While Alaric Chapin and his fellow soldiers were paid as little as $13 a month, the enlisted crew of ships like the USS *Gettysburg* could earn $500 or even $1,000 for capturing a blockade runner. Prize money for officers could run into the thousands of dollars. During the Civil War, more than $25 million was paid out in prize money.

POWDER SHIP

Following the failed first infantry assault on Fort Fisher, Admiral David Porter developed a plan to blow a hole in the seaward side of the fort by loading a ship with thousands of pounds of gunpowder and exploding it under the fort's walls. Lamson courageously volunteered to pilot the powder ship into position. Two days before Christmas 1864, the USS *Louisiana* was packed with two hundred tons of black powder and rigged for towing. Lamson was placed in command of the USS *Wilderness* and assigned to tow the powder ship as close to the enemy fort as possible. Lamson guided the tandem ships well within range of Confederate guns, the blackness of night offering the only protection from being spotted by the enemy. Just before midnight, within three hundred yards of Fort Fisher, Lamson cut loose the *Louisiana* while its crew of volunteers lit timing fuses on the powder kegs. Among the valiant volunteers onboard the *Louisiana* was Lieutenant Samuel Preston, who had graduated first in the navy class of 1862, just ahead of Lamson. At the very last survivable moment, Preston and his crew mates boarded a small boat and rowed like madmen back to the safety of the *Wilderness*. Lamson described the *Louisiana* explosion as an "immense column of flame with four distinct reports like heavy thunder," after which a "dense mass of smoke enveloped everything." As spectacular as the blast was, the fortress was soundly built, and the damage was not extensive enough to ignite the fort's powder magazine and cave Fisher's outer walls. The morning after their heroics, former classmates Lamson and Preston were reunited at breakfast with Admiral Porter on the Union flagship.

Fort Fisher would be taken by storm. General Alfred Terry devised a three-pronged plan to seize the fort: First, an infantry division of U.S. Colored Troops would engage the Confederate troops outside Fort Fisher to prevent the Rebels from reinforcing the fort. Second, sailors and marines from Porter's fleet would make an amphibious landing and assault the fort from the beach. Third, in a coordinated attack, Union infantry would storm Fort Fisher from land. Protecting the fort from land assault was an extensive palisade, a nine-foot-high solid fence made from logs set on end and lashed together with heavy rope. A squad of volunteers was recruited to advance before the column and, using axes, cut through the ropes and timbers, creating a breach in the palisades and allowing Northern troops to storm the fort.

OPENING A BLOODY GATE

Alaric Chapin, the teenage farm boy from upstate New York, was one of thirteen soldiers who volunteered to chop through the palisade. Chapin had been sixteen years old in 1864 when he told the recruiting officer his age was eighteen and enlisted in the 142nd New York State Infantry. Chapin's enlistment papers included a physical description: brown hair, blue eyes, fair complexion and five feet, ten inches in height (tall in a day when the average male stood five feet, six inches). Now, less than a year later and still under the legal enlistment age, Chapin was a seasoned veteran. He had been promoted to corporal of Company G and had fought with the 142nd New York in the Battles of Cold Harbor, Petersburg and New Market Heights, where his feet froze in the Virginia mud. His patriotism and sense of duty called him to volunteer for the perilous mission in which he was about to engage. Volunteering along with Chapin was his best friend, Jimmy Spring, his comrade in Company G. Like Chapin, Spring was from upstate New York, and he, too, had overstated his age to fight for the Union. Chapin and Spring, muskets slung on their backs, axes in hand, waited with eleven compatriots for the order to advance. At two o'clock in the afternoon, the navy guns fell silent. It was time to move forward. Creeping along the ground for almost three hundred yards, the thirteen volunteers reached the enemy palisade unobserved. Concentrating their axe blows on the lashing ropes, and using shovels and battering rams to loosen and then topple some of the posts, they cut openings in the palisades. Because of the breach they had opened, the volunteers came under fire from two Rebel cannons positioned at the front of the fort. The axe men had chopped open a bloody gate, and nine thousand Union soldiers poured through to engage the enemy.

While Chapin and Spring were attacking the palisade with their axes, the beach assault began. U.S. Marines, armed with rifles, were the first to land. The marine mission was to provide covering fire while the sailors who landed next converged on the fort. From the *Gettysburg*, Lamson led a storming party of seventy blue jackets, enlisted sailors nicknamed for the uniforms they wore. The sailors, armed with drawn pistols and cutlasses, were to storm the fort and fight their way over the walls in hand-to-hand combat. Like Lamson, all of the navy officers had gone into battle wearing dress uniforms, and as they charged, the navy men cheered loudly. Next to Lamson, leading the assault party from the USS *Malvern* was Lieutenant Preston. While the marine riflemen tried to keep the defenders of the fort off the ramparts, Lamson, Preston and the other navy officers led the charge up the beach but were hit with withering canister fire from the fort's cannons. Many of the charging attackers pulled their blue caps low over their eyes so as not to see the flashes of the enemy guns. The sailors were not trained in infantry tactics, and the assault became an unorganized mess. The marines failed to keep up their covering fire and joined the charge. Of the two thousand sailors who landed on the beach, no more than two hundred made it to the walls of the fort, but that number included all of the officers.

As the blue jackets approached the fort, North Carolina troops poured volley after volley of musket fire into the sailors. Preston, running next to Lamson, was shot in the groin and fell facedown. No more than twenty paces from where Preston fell, musket balls struck Lamson in the left shoulder and arm, knocking him to the sand. The wounded Lamson crawled to where his classmate lay, but as the blue jackets rolled Preston on his back,

Lamson could see his friend was already dead. The musket ball had severed the femoral artery in Preston's left thigh, and he had quickly bled to death without regaining consciousness. Lamson rose to his feet and resumed the fight, but while pistols and cutlasses may be suitable for boarding an enemy vessel, they are woefully inadequate for assaulting entrenched infantry. One sailor remarked, "We might as well have had broom sticks" for all the good the swords did. The few marines and sailors, including the wounded Lamson, who reached the walls of the garrison were pinned down below the sand cliffs under Fort Fisher. The Carolinians taunted the attackers by hooting and catcalling for the sailors to come on up and fight. To provide some protection for his sailors who were pinned down on the beach, Porter ordered the fleet to resume the bombardment of the fort. Lamson and his remaining men were trapped under the enemy guns until dark.

Although unsuccessful, the navy's beach assault kept the Confederates busy on one side of the fort and gave the army time to exploit their breach on the land side of the garrison. As Union troops, led by his own New York regiment, poured through the breach he had created, Spring was shot in the head by a Confederate rifleman. He died instantly. Chapin, seeing his friend fall, threw down his axe, unstrapped his musket, fixed his bayonet and joined the bloody hand-to-hand struggle. The inside of the fort was a killing ground; the fighting lasted more than six hours. Long after darkness fell, with most of the senior Confederate officers dead or wounded, Fort Fisher, the last great bastion of the Carolina Sounds, surrendered. The Rebels had lost 600 dead, with 1,500 more captured along with the fort. The Union lost 1,300 men. Among those killed were 6 from the USS *Gettysburg*. The ship also had 6 of its men, including Lamson, severely wounded.

With the capture of Fort Fisher, the Union army could directly attack Wilmington, which fell a month later. Two months after the fall of Wilmington cut his supply lines, Lee surrendered his army in Virginia. General Adelbert Ames, commander of the Union division that breached the Confederate palisades at Fort Fisher, recommended Chapin and all thirteen volunteer axe men for the Medal of Honor. Unfortunately, in the aftermath of the battle, Ames's report was misplaced, and his recommendation never made it to the War Department.

Lamson recovered sufficiently from his wounds to return to duty as captain of the *Gettysburg*. Peace brought an end to the taking of enemy ships and the lucrative prize money that accompanied their capture. After the fleet toured European ports in 1866, Lamson resigned from the navy and married his pen pal, cousin Kate Buckingham. In 1870, Lamson brought his bride home to Oregon, where the publicity of his wartime exploits had made him a local celebrity.

Chapin mustered out of the army on June 7, 1865, eleven days shy of his eighteenth birthday. He returned home to New York and then headed west with his parents, who had bought a farm near River Falls, Wisconsin. On April 6, 1871, Chapin married Mary Smith and bought his own farm, where he and his wife raised three sons and two daughters. After thirty years of farming in Wisconsin, Chapin moved his family to a new farm near the tiny Minnesota hamlet of Workman Township.

MEDAL OF HONOR ARRIVES IN THE MAIL

The Gillespie design of the Medal of Honor was adopted in 1904. Alaric Chapin received his Medal of Honor in the mail. *Library of Congress.*

Forty-nine years after the end of the Civil War, Bruce Anderson, one of the thirteen volunteers who chopped through the palisading at Fort Fisher, hired a lawyer to petition Congress for the Medal of Honor. Anderson's attorney convinced the adjutant general of the army to launch an investigation, which uncovered General Ames's letter of recommendation. The army then launched a search for the surviving volunteers. In addition to Anderson, three other volunteers, including Chapin, were still alive and were awarded the medal. A letter from the War Department was delivered to Chapin's Minnesota farm in early January 1915. Almost fifty years to the day after the desperate fight for Fort Fisher, two typewritten paragraphs on government stationery informed the sixty-seven-year-old grandfather that he had been awarded the Congressional Medal of Honor. The medal arrived a few days later in a separate parcel, and Chapin took great pride in the golden medal with the blue ribbon and frequently wore it in public, especially to his GAR meetings.

Sixteen U.S. sailors were awarded the Medal of Honor for gallantry in the assault against Fort Fisher, but there would be no medal for Lieutenant Lamson. His bravery under fire and his heroic charge on the Carolina beach are unquestionable feats of valor, but unlike their army counterparts, navy officers were not eligible for the Medal of Honor, a rule that remained in effect until World War I.

VETERANS MOVE TO PORTLAND

Upon his return to Oregon, Lamson briefly worked his father's farm. He never achieved the fortune he dreamed of, but his fame landed him appointment to a number of government positions. He was appointed as the county clerk of Yamhill County in 1873 and later taught mathematics at Pacific University in Forest Grove. In 1877, Judge Matthew Deady appointed Lamson to serve as clerk of the U.S. District Court in Portland.

Kate Lamson would bear seven children, but sadly, all but two would die before reaching adulthood. Kate passed away in 1893 at the age of forty-nine. Following his wife's death, Lamson's health deteriorated from old battle wounds and malaria contracted during the war. He retired from the court in 1894 and petitioned for a military disability pension. In 1895, in recognition of his wartime heroism, the U.S. Navy recommissioned Lamson and placed him on its retired list, entitling Lamson to draw a pension. Lamson was a member of Portland's GAR Post 13, but his illness kept him largely confined to his home. Lamson died in 1903.

Lamson's death was front-page news in the *Morning Oregonian*. The newspaper printed a lengthy summary of Lamson's navy exploits and included a four- by six-inch picture of the distinguished officer. Lamson was well known in Portland and held in the highest esteem by all who met him. At his funeral, Lamson's coffin was covered with the bullet-riddled flag from the USS *Mount Washington*. He was laid to rest in Portland's River View Cemetery, next to his wife and four of his children. Lamson's ability and courage were praised in Admiral Porter's memoirs. A collection of his wartime correspondence, letters to and from his father, his fiancée and other contemporaries, has been published in the book *Lamson of the Gettysburg: The Civil War Letters of Lieutenant Roswell H. Lamson, U.S. Navy*, edited by James and Patricia McPherson. Three U.S. Navy ships, including a World War II destroyer, have been named in Lamson's honor.

Alaric Chapin. *Glenbow Museum.*

After a half century of working the land, his children pursuing their own careers, Alaric Chapin decided it was time to retire from farming. Chapin and his wife, Mary, traveled first to Canada to visit eldest son Orris in Calgary. Then they moved to Oregon, where their two younger sons lived. Earl Chapin was the proprietor of a Portland grocery store, while youngest son Arthur worked as a bridgeman for the railroad. Like Lamson, Chapin was a member of the GAR, and in Portland he joined Post 21. Nearly sixty years after the fall of Fort Fisher, on Thanksgiving Day 1924, Alaric Chapin passed to history at his home located at 1452 Cleveland Avenue in Portland. His funeral notice made no mention of the Medal of Honor, only that the GAR would oversee the funeral service. Chapin was laid to rest in Rose City Cemetery. Chapin's granddaughter, Miriam Adams, donated his Medal of Honor and his musket and bayonet to the Glenbow Museum in Calgary, Alberta.

Alaric Chapin and Roswell Lamson never met in life. The tall teenager and the dashing officer fought valiantly for the Union on a sand spit in North Carolina on a winter afternoon in 1865. They both saw good friends die at their side. But Lamson and Chapin had attacked from opposite sides of the Rebel fortress, and their lives took different courses after that day. Chapin did not arrive in Oregon until long after Lamson had passed to the ages. Yet the bones of the heroes of Fort Fisher rest just eight miles apart in separate Portland cemeteries. Perhaps they have met in heaven and recounted their adventures to the angels.

A Quaker Civil War Hero

Buried on a Mountaintop in Agness, Oregon

The old soldier came to Oregon late in life. Fleeing Philadelphia for a better climate for his ailing wife, Nathan Edgerton staked a homestead along the Rogue River in a remote southwest corner of Oregon. At seventy-one years of age, with several careers behind him, Edgerton began to build a farm that within ten years would have a small house, sixteen feet by twenty feet in size with a twelve- by twenty-foot addition; a woodshed and a chicken house; twenty head of sheep; over twenty acres of orchards with peach, almond and apple trees; several stands of bees that annually produced more than two hundred pounds of honey; and, sadly, the grave of his wife, Esther. The house itself was modestly furnished in the efficient style of a Quaker farmer. In an upstairs bedroom was stored a blue army uniform, a bullet-riddled flag, an old sword and Nathan Edgerton's most prized possession: his Congressional Medal of Honor.

The Edgerton farm is located near Agness, an Oregon community that even today has a population of just 113 souls and still receives mail by jet boat from Gold Beach. Nathan and Esther Edgerton came west in 1909 after two of their sons had followed the Oregon Trail.

Nathan Huntley Edgerton was born on August 28, 1838, in eastern Ohio. He was raised on his parents' farm and educated in the Quaker tradition. The only newspaper allowed in the home was *The Friend*, a Quaker journal still published today. When Edgerton was about eight years old, one of his chores was to walk the two miles from the farm to Warren, Ohio, to take shoes to the local cobbler shop for repair. It was at the shoemaker's store that young Nathan learned from a local newspaper that the United States was at war with Mexico. Never mentioning a word of the newspaper to his father, Nathan looked forward to each trip to town, where he could learn more about the generals and the battles being fought. He became greatly interested in military affairs.

When he turned twenty-one, Edgerton left home to enroll in the Friends School at Westtown, Pennsylvania. There he took up a course of study in the classics, English and engineering. After his second year of college, Edgerton became an instructor at the school, and by his third year, he was a full professor and the chair of the Chemistry Department. Professor Edgerton would have likely led a pastoral life of research and teaching at the Quaker college had war not altered the course of his life.

Despite his boyhood fascination with military affairs, Edgerton stayed true to his pacifist upbringing and did not join the army at the start of the Civil War. That changed in the summer of 1863, when the Confederate army entered Pennsylvania and Governor Andrew Curtain issued a call for sixty thousand volunteers to repel the invaders. Edgerton resigned from the faculty and traveled to the capital of Harrisburg, where he joined the 29th Pennsylvania Militia. After less than two weeks of military training, the volunteers were marched to Gettysburg.

The emergency troops were stationed just north of Gettysburg on the road to Harrisburg. Their mission was twofold: First, in case of a Confederate victory, they were to prevent Lee from marching on the state capital. Second, they were to act as a protective screen for the Army of the Potomac in case Jeb Stuart's Rebel cavalry tried to attack the Union rear. For three hot and dusty days, Edgerton kept up a rearguard action while he could hear the roar of the biggest battle fought on American soil happening just a few miles away. On the Fourth of July 1863, Lee's men retreated back into Virginia, and Pennsylvania was rid of the invader. Edgerton and the rest of the militia troops were mustered out of the service at the end of July.

Returning to the Friends School was not an option for a military man, so Edgerton enrolled in Philadelphia Polytechnic College. By the end of the summer, he had passed the courses in military engineering and desired an appointment as lieutenant of engineers in the regular army. The head of the college wrote on Edgerton's behalf to Secretary of War Edwin Stanton and recommended a commission for his student. Stanton replied that only West Point could appoint officers of engineers and that the army's greatest need was for line officers. Stanton invited Edgerton to present himself to Colonel Casey at Washington, D.C., for examination as an officer. The Board of Examiners was so impressed with Edgerton's knowledge and ability that he was commissioned as a first lieutenant in the regular army on September 14, 1863.

CONGRESS AUTHORIZES BLACK REGIMENTS

Lieutenant Edgerton was ordered back to Philadelphia, where ten regiments of African American volunteers were being organized. Only white men were allowed to serve as officers, and Edgerton was appointed second in command of Company H, 6th U.S. Colored Infantry. After two months of drill and training, ten thousand free black men of the Union army marched through the streets of Philadelphia. Thousands of citizens came out to cheer the colored brigade as they marched to the railroad station and boarded a train for Delaware.

Disembarking from the train, Edgerton and his men boarded a navy ship for transport to Virginia. The 6th was assigned to the XVIII Corps and set up a garrison camp south of Yorktown. For the next six months, Edgerton's soldiers performed fatigue duty and manual labor, stood guard watch and manned picket lines. They were sent out on a few raids, mostly in support of white cavalry, but were kept out of major combat operations. Many senior officers and politicians did not support the use of black troops in actual fighting.

In May 1864, all of the black regiments in the XVIII Corps were consolidated into one division, the only African American division in the Union army. The Army of the James was commanded by General Benjamin Butler, a political appointee and a mediocre commander but a champion for the use of black men in combat. At dawn on May 5, 150 transport boats waited on the James River to take the thirty-five thousand men under Butler's command to attack Confederate positions at City Point and Bermuda Hundred. Although the colored division performed well, the overall campaign was a failure, and Butler was forced to withdraw his army.

The colored division was again transported upriver to Petersburg, where Grant was laying siege to the entrenched Rebels outside the city. In one of several Union attacks on the fortifications, Edgerton was ordered to warn the guards of a pontoon bridge that an engagement was about to commence and to be prepared to pull the bridge across the river should Confederates attempt to cross.

African American soldiers in Virginia. *Library of Congress.*

Having completed his mission, Edgerton, mounted on horseback, intended to return to Union headquarters, but while he was at the river, Confederate troops had advanced their position. Without knowing it, the solitary horseman had ridden through a gap in the gray line and found himself between the main body of Rebels and their advance skirmishers. Realizing his predicament, the officer spurred his horse and escaped at a full gallop while a volley of musket balls buzzed like bees as they flew past his head, missing both rider and mount entirely.

UNION PLAN BLOWS UP

After two months and six assaults failed to take Petersburg, Union general Ambrose Burnside came up with a new plan. A mine would be dug twenty feet under the Confederate fortifications, where explosives would be placed to blow open the ramparts. While the five-hundred-foot-long tunnel was being constructed, the Colored Division was being trained to lead the Union assault. Engineers knew that the explosion would create a huge crater in the ground. Two lead regiments of black soldiers were specially trained to circle around the crater on both sides in a two-pronged attack that would create a gateway for the rest of the division that was to burst through and seize the main road into Petersburg.

All was ready when eight thousand pounds of gunpowder were placed in the mine. The day before the attack, Burnside's superior, General George Meade, decided not to use black troops in the assault. Meade felt that if the attack went poorly, there would be political repercussions in the North. Burnside appealed to Grant, but Grant sided with Meade. When no general would volunteer his men for the assault, a replacement division of white soldiers was chosen by lot, while the trained black men were ordered to the rear.

On July 30, 1864, Lieutenant Edgerton was serving on the brigade staff and had reported for duty at 3:00 a.m. Edgerton would relate in later years that at 4:45 a.m., the earth seemed to slip under his feet, and he felt more than heard the shock wave of a thunderous explosion. The mine had been detonated, and tons of earth was blown into the sky. A massive crater—170 feet long, 80 feet wide and 30 feet deep—was left in the ground. The white division chosen to lead the attack charged gallantly, but instead of traversing the perimeter of the crater as the colored troops had trained for, they rushed into the depression. Confederate defenders rallied to the edge of the crater and began firing muskets and artillery down on the Union boys in a slaughter they called a turkey shoot. Grant called it "the saddest affair I have witnessed in the war." General Burnside was blamed for the failure and relieved of his command.

CHAFFIN'S FARM

General Butler ached for his colored regiments to prove themselves in a major campaign, and he got his chance in late September. The Army of the James was once again loaded on transports that steamed downriver to attack entrenched Confederate fortifications on New Market Heights. The colored division was assigned to the left of the Union line in an area known as Chaffin's Farm. Edgerton's 6th U.S. and the 4th U.S. formed the brigade that would attack the center of the Rebel line manned by a division of battle-hardened Texans who were reinforced by cavalry and artillery.

With a dense fog obscuring the attack preparations, the Union regiments formed battle lines at 4:30 a.m. Each company formed in two ranks behind its captain. Behind the rear rank stood the lieutenants and sergeants to keep the men in line and to serve as file closers should gaps open. Behind the infantry, mounted on horseback, was the regimental staff that included Edgerton, who had been appointed as regimental adjutant. At the head of each regiment, in the center of the line, were the regimental colors: a red, white and blue national flag and the blue battle flag unique to the regiment. The center of the hand-painted silk regimental standard of the 6th U.S. Colored Infantry portrayed Lady Liberty presenting the U.S. flag to a black soldier under the motto "Freedom for All."

On September 29, 1864, with their flags leading the way, the attack commenced at dawn. As a brilliant sun burned away the fog, the Union men forded a stream under withering fire of Texas muskets, but they continued to advance. The Confederates had erected abatis, or barriers, to block the enemy advance, but pioneers—specially trained troops equipped with axes, picks and shovels—came forward and cleared the obstructions, and the colored brigade continued their charge. Nathan Edgerton's horse was shot from beneath him, so the lieutenant drew his sword and advanced on foot. The entire color guard of the 6th U.S. was shot down, and the flags lay on the ground. Captain Charles York of Company B retrieved the regimental flag but was shot dead. Other men raised the national flag only to suffer the same fate as York. Edgerton watched as his friend Lieutenant Frederick Meyer lifted the regimental colors only to be struck in the heart. The line of brave black men continued to advance even without their beloved banners to signal the way.

Edgerton reached the slain color guard and pried the regiment's blue flag from Meyer's hands. With the flag in his left hand and his sword in his right, Edgerton hurried up the hill to restore the flag to its place in front of the regiment. After advancing but a few yards, he was slammed to the ground. Thinking his boots had tangled in the underbrush, Edgerton leapt to his feet and found the flagstaff had broken in two pieces. Reaching for the flag, he found he could not lift it, for a musket ball had struck his left wrist, shattering the bone before splitting the flagpole. Edgerton sheathed his sword, grasped the broken flag with his good right hand and rushed to the front of the regiment. At about the same time, Sergeant Alexander Kelly of Company F arrived with the national colors. The men of the 6th rallied on the flags and re-formed for another assault, but the brigade had been shot to pieces. There were too few able men to be effective. The commanding officer wisely

Medal of Honor recipient Nathan Edgerton is buried on his homestead near Agness, Oregon. *Courtesy of Nancy Edgerton-Ahlstrom Anders-Sterle.*

ordered the men to retreat back across the stream. The 6th U.S. Colored Infantry suffered 209 casualties that day, and its brigade partner, the 4th U.S., lost 178 men.

Other brigades from the colored division broke the Rebel line, and the Union won the field of battle. It was General Butler's great victory of the war, and no one could doubt the skill and courage of African Americans in battle. Butler wrote, "A few more such gallant charges and to command Colored Troops will be the post of honor in the American armies."

Only twenty-five Medals of Honor were awarded to black soldiers and sailors in the Civil War. Fourteen of those medals were awarded for gallantry in the heavy fighting at Chaffin's Farm. Among the African American recipients of the Medal of Honor was Alexander Kelly, the sergeant who rescued the national flag. Kelly received his decoration on April 6, 1865. After the war, Butler's fame would earn him three terms in the U.S. Congress and the governorship of Massachusetts.

HOSPITAL AND MARRIAGE

The wounded Edgerton was taken to a field hospital and then transferred to the Chesapeake Officer's Hospital, where surgeons successfully operated to save his arm. The *New York Tribune* mentioned Edgerton's heroics in its account of the battle, and General Butler personally ordered that Edgerton be promoted to captain.

Captain Edgerton was given leave to return to Philadelphia to convalesce. While on leave, the newly promoted captain married his fiancée, Esther Mendenhall. When fit for duty, Edgerton was ordered to

Harrisburg to serve as a judge in court-martial proceedings against one hundred or so Copperheads accused of aiding the enemy.

Edgerton was in Harrisburg when he learned of the assassination of President Lincoln. As Lincoln's body was transported from Washington to Springfield, Illinois, it would lay in state in the state capitols along the route. When the president's body was lying in state in the Pennsylvania capitol, Captain Edgerton had the distinction of being in the honor guard. Shortly after this duty, Edgerton was ordered to rejoin his regiment, where he was given command of Company H. The 6th U.S. Colored Infantry mustered out of the army on September 20, 1865, and at his new bride's insistence, the military career of Nathan Edgerton came to an end.

The twenty-seven-year-old Edgerton began his civilian career as a conductor on the Reading Railroad but was soon promoted to the office of the general manager. He left the railroad to become an assistant manager for the James W. Queen Company of Philadelphia, manufacturer of scientific instruments. He left Queen to become manager of the Braun Electric Light Company. He assisted in the introduction of electric power to Pennsylvania and New England and held several patents for his inventions, which included one of the first electric motors available to the public.

Edgerton became a member of the Franklin Institute and served as a board member on the Committee of Arts and Sciences for more than twenty-five years. He was an exhibitor at the Centennial Exhibition in Philadelphia, the Paris Exhibition of 1878 and the World Industrial and Cotton Centennial in New Orleans in 1884 and 1885. At each of these conventions, Edgerton was awarded medals for his inventions, which included electrical, optical and scientific instruments. In 1898, he became president of the High Tension Electric Storage Company, which manufactured electrical batteries.

CONGRESSIONAL MEDAL OF HONOR

On March 22, 1898, Nathan H. Edgerton, former captain of the 6th United States Colored Infantry, was notified by the War Department that "by the direction of the President of the United States and under the provisions of the Act of Congress approved March 3, 1863, a Congressional Medal of Honor has this day been presented to you for most distinguished gallantry in action." Thirty-four years after he had lifted his regiment's flag from the blood-soaked Virginia soil, one of Edgerton's fellow officers, Captain Robert Beath, had recalled Edgerton's valor and nominated him for the medal.

Nathan and Esther Edgerton had three sons and a daughter. The couple left the sophistication of Philadelphia for a rustic life on the Rogue River. The Edgertons were together for ten happy years in Oregon until Esther passed away in 1919. Shortly after his son Edward took down his life story, Nathan Edgerton passed to the ages on October 27, 1932. He rests next to his wife of fifty-five years on the top of a mountain on the old homestead.

Son of the Prophet

John Brown's Last Son Dies in Portland

May 10, 1919, was one of those delightful spring days that Oregon is famous for: a warm and dry Monday nestled within a month of splendid early summer weather. Salmon Brown, the last surviving son of Captain John Brown of Kansas and Harpers Ferry fame, was living in Portland. Sixty years after his father was hanged for attempting to incite a slave rebellion, Salmon Brown took his gun, placed the cold steel barrel to his temple and pulled the trigger.

Salmon Brown was born in Hudson, Ohio, on October 2, 1836. The Brown family was large, even by nineteenth-century standards. John Brown's first wife gave birth to six healthy children before dying after delivering a stillborn seventh child. Brown then married sixteen-year-old Mary Ann Day, who would give him thirteen more children, including her third child, Salmon. Of the twenty children fathered by John Brown, eleven survived to adulthood. His seven sons became trusted lieutenants in the crusade against slavery.

John Brown was a strict father and a deeply religious man. One time when young Salmon was having difficulty reciting his Bible lesson, his father tried to squeeze the devil out of him. Brown clutched his son so violently that Salmon nearly died. Despite his religious fervor, John Brown did not belong to an organized church. He believed that no man's interpretation of scripture was greater than that of any other man.

In his search for success, John Brown moved his family often. He tried different business ventures, including leather tanning, surveying, cattle trading and sheep farming. It was this last occupation that brought Brown

John Brown. *Library of Congress.*

acclaim and financial success as a businessman. Brown was a champion sheep breeder and founded a wool marketing cooperative in Ohio.

The 1837 murder of abolitionist Elijah Lovejoy by proslavery partisans forever changed the course of the Brown family's life. John Brown publicly vowed: "Here, before God, in the presence of these witnesses, from this time, I consecrate my life to the destruction of slavery!" From that moment, the Brown family was committed to abolition. They ran their own militant version of the Underground Railroad, guiding escaped slaves to sanctuary in Canada. Occasionally, the Browns would conduct armed incursions into slave states, forcibly liberating slaves from their masters.

Brown believed fervently in abolition, but unlike many of his contemporaries, he also believed in equality and mixing of the races, and he practiced what he preached. In the late 1840s, a community of free people of color was founded near Lake Placid in North Elba, New York. Brown moved his family to North Elba to live among those he fought to set free.

BLOODY KANSAS

In the mid-1850s, "Kansas Fever" swept the nation as the territory opened to settlement. Salmon Brown and four of his brothers caught the fever and were determined to build their own legacies on the prairie. The Brown brothers wanted to peacefully develop their homestead, but they were soon caught up in the violent turmoil of the region. Under the Kansas-Nebraska Act, settlers would decide if Kansas was to become a free state or a slave state.

When the day of the election came, five thousand armed Missourians called Border Ruffians rode into the territory, seized polling places and elected a proslavery legislature. President Pierce backed the proslavery government. The Free Soilers responded by electing a separate legislature that met in Topeka. John Brown Jr. was elected as a free state delegate.

In 1855, John Jr. wrote to his father for assistance. He pleaded that the Kansas settlers were being terrorized by the Missouri ruffians and that they needed guns more than they needed bread. In response to his son's plea, John Brown joined his boys in Kansas. Upon his arrival, Brown was appalled at what he found. His sons and their wives all lived in a single shack; they were starving and shivering with fever. Brown went to work, and within three weeks, he had built a sturdy cabin. He built another, and soon there stood a small but thriving community near Pottawatomie Creek known as Brown's Station.

With his health regained, John Brown Jr. formed a free state militia known as the Pottawatomie Rifles. When word came that Border Ruffians were riding toward Lawrence, Brown's jayhawker militia moved out to support the town. John Brown Sr. accompanied his sons. On the way to Lawrence, the militia learned that the Ruffians had sacked the town and burned the hotel. Not a single resident had fired a shot in his own self-defense, and this outraged the elder Brown, who declared, "Something must be done to show these barbarians that we, too, have rights."

Old Man Brown told his sons and a few selected men to prepare for a secret mission. John Brown Jr. cautioned his father against doing anything rash and refused to go with him, but brothers Salmon, Frederick, Owen and Oliver joined the old man. The party was also joined by two of the Pottawatomie men. Their target was Dutch Henry Sherman, a leader of the proslavery Law and Order Party.

Brown armed his men with broadswords he had purchased with funds donated by abolitionists. The swords were short with a stout base and resembled the gladiator swords of ancient Rome. The army issued them to artillery crews for self-defense. On the night of May 24, 1856, the Brown party called at the cabin of James Doyle and ordered everyone outside. There were five people in the cabin: Doyle, his wife and three sons. The Browns took Doyle and his two adult sons away but left a sixteen-year-old son with his mother. The Doyles had been professional slave catchers before settling in Kansas, and as the men were led away, Mrs. Doyle cried out that their devilment had brought this fate upon them. The Doyles were led to a creek bed, where Owen and Salmon Brown set upon them with the swords. The work was swift, violent and bloody. The Doyles raised their arms in self-defense, but the strong blades of the broadswords sliced through flesh and bone, severing limbs and smashing skulls. When the horrible work was done, Salmon and Owen washed the blood from their blades, and John Brown fired a pistol ball into the head of the elder Doyle, making sure he was dead.

The Browns then went to the cabin of proslavery settler Allen Wilkinson and ordered him outside. The grisly murder was repeated, but this time it was the two men from the Pottawatomie Rifles doing the hacking and stabbing. The Browns then visited a third cabin and took out three men, including William Sherman, the brother of the Dutch Henry Sherman whom John Brown was seeking. Upon questioning, Sherman's companions convinced Brown that they had taken no part in the violence against the free state settlers. They were released, but Sherman was led away and slaughtered like the four men before him. Later in life, Salmon Brown denied taking part in the actual killings, saying the militia men had done the deed, but the weight of the evidence puts a bloody sword in his hand.

Because of the infamous Pottawatomie Massacre, John Brown became a national figure with a price on his head. John Brown Jr. broke with his father over the killings and resigned from the Pottawatomie Rifles. Later, John Jr. and his brother Jason, who did not participate in the murders, were captured by proslavery forces, severely beaten and thrown in prison. Frederick Brown, who was involved in the massacre, was shot and killed by Border Ruffians. Brown's Station was burned to the ground.

In retaliation, John Brown led a free state militia in an attack on a proslavery force camped along a spring on the Santa Fe Trail. For over three hours, one hundred armed men exchanged deadly fire in what became known as the Battle of Black Jack. The clash is considered by many historians as the first battle of the Civil War. Brown's men were victorious, and he held several Missouri men hostage until they promised to release his imprisoned sons. Salmon Brown was wounded in the battle, and his father took Salmon to Nebraska to recover. John Brown returned to the fighting in Kansas, but Salmon Brown, once his war wounds healed, took his wife and returned to the family farm in New York.

FATHER AND BROTHERS LOST AT HARPERS FERRY

The free soil men prevailed in Kansas, and John Brown took the fight against slavery to other states. His plans became grandiose as he dreamed of founding a republic of freed slaves somewhere in the South. He sought support from leading men like William Lloyd Garrison and Frederick Douglass and received financing from a clique of wealthy northern businessmen known as the Secret Six. Douglass argued against violence even as Brown was plotting to seize the federal armory at Harpers Ferry, Virginia. His plan was to arm local slaves and march south, recruiting an army of liberation.

Brown envisioned leading a brigade of 4,500 followers, but in the end he attacked the arsenal with just 21 men, including sons Owen, Watson and Oliver. Salmon Brown did not take part in the raid. Once Brown's raiders captured the armory building, nothing went right. The raiders were quickly surrounded by townspeople and local militia and were trapped inside a brick engine house. They held out for two days until the building was stormed by one hundred marines led by army colonel Robert E. Lee. John Brown was severely wounded and captured. Brown's sons Watson and Oliver were killed, along with many of his raiders. Owen Brown and a few others escaped.

John Brown was put on trial for treason in nearby Charles Town. Despite northern pleas to spare his life, Brown was hanged on December 2, 1859. Ralph Waldo Emerson wrote that Brown would make "the gallows glorious like the Cross." Among those witnessing the execution were Walt Whitman, Thomas "Stonewall" Jackson and John Wilkes Booth. Six of Brown's raiders followed him to the scaffold.

In one of his final letters from prison, Brown wrote, "I am now quite certain that the crimes of this guilty land will never be purged away but with blood." As Brown prophesized, the nation was soon engaged in a great civil war.

In his last will and testament, Brown decreed that a new Bible be purchased for each of his children, and he specified that five dollars for each Bible be set aside to procure them from the finest store in Boston or New York. Brown's eldest son, John Jr., was to receive his surveying compass; Jason was willed his father's silver watch; his rifle was to go to Owen; and Salmon Brown was to receive fifty dollars cash.

With his father and three of his brothers dead, and another brother a fugitive, the burden of running the family farm in New York fell to Salmon. Despite many well-wishers and promises of financial support, the reality was that the Brown family was impoverished. As the nation mobilized troops for the Civil War, Captain James Fairman was authorized to raise a regiment of volunteers from upstate New York. Fairman, an admirer of John Brown, made the journey to North Elba, where he visited Salmon Brown and offered him a commission as an officer. Fairman had been previously unsuccessful in recruiting a regiment, and his promotion to colonel was contingent upon enlisting the one thousand men required to fill the muster rolls. Fairman believed serving with the son of John Brown would entice other men to join his regiment.

Brown accepted the offer and was commissioned a lieutenant in Company K of the 96th New York Infantry. A lieutenant in those days earned $105 per month (compared to $13 for a private), money that would ease the burden of Brown's mother and sisters. The 96th Regiment trained in New York for three weeks and then was sent south to join General McClellan's Army of the Potomac.

While the common soldiers of the Union army may have admired John Brown, the so-called gentlemen officers of the 96th were not so keen on serving with the son of the prophet. The officers signed a petition stating that they were not against Brown "as a man or citizen, but they did not wish to associate with a man having the notoriety that said Brown has in our country." The officers feared that the regiment might be especially targeted by Rebel troops if it became known that John Brown's son was in their ranks. The petitioners asked Colonel Fairman to remove Brown from the regiment.

Not wanting to distract from the war effort, Lieutenant Salmon Brown resigned from the Union army. As his regiment marched off to war singing "John Brown's body lies a-mouldering in the grave his soul is marching on!" Salmon Brown went home to North Elba. Outraged over the regiment's treatment of Brown, William Lloyd Garrison published the names of the officers who had signed the petition in his newspaper, the *Liberator*. Garrison wanted to guarantee that "the names of those who had scorned the son of John Brown would be handed down in history!"

Returning to the family farm, Brown decided to quit the East Coast forever and start a new life in the West. In 1864, he packed all his worldly goods in a covered wagon and, with his wife, Abbie, their three daughters, his mother and three of his sisters, headed for California.

Danger on the Oregon Trail

Fearful of Sioux raiding parties, the Brown family joined a party of eighty wagons from Missouri for the trip across the plains. Brown was looking for safety in numbers, but as it turned out, he had as much to fear from his traveling companions as he did from the native peoples. They had not traveled far when Brown was told that the Missouri men had not forgotten the border war or his part in the Kansas violence. As the wagon train prepared to stop for the night, Brown kept his team hitched. Sure enough, he was approached by a group of armed men who told him they had some business with him. Brown had his gun ready for instant use and told the men that he was taking his wagon over the next rise to set up camp. The Missouri men told him to go on and get his family situated and they would see him later that evening.

Brown drove his wagon over the crest and didn't stop. He traveled throughout the night and didn't halt until four o'clock in the morning, when he came across a wagon train from Indiana. The Hoosier train was pro-Union and welcomed the Brown party into their group. Desiring to avoid confrontation with the Missourians, the Indiana party broke camp before dawn and continued on the trail.

It was common practice for wagon trains to stop on Sundays to rest and graze their livestock, hold religious services and perform needed repairs. Brown's new companions were doing just that when lookouts spotted the Missouri wagons cresting a hill in the distance and headed straight at them. The Indiana party rushed to their wagons, and over the next several weeks, a slow-speed oxen-pulled wagon chase took place across plains and mountains as the Missouri train tried to overtake the Hoosiers and dispense some border justice to Salmon Brown.

Brown and his companions reached the army fort at Soda Springs and stayed there until the pursuing train arrived. The army officers questioned the Missouri men and asked if they were Union men or Rebels. "Union men" was the response, so the army asked if they would prove it by taking the Oath of Allegiance to the United States. The Missourians objected. Some of the men had served under Confederate general Sterling Price and said they did not want to take sides again; they just wanted to leave the war behind and start a new life. The army refused to relent and forced every man in the Missouri wagon train to take the oath.

At Soda Springs, one of the Missouri men admitted to Brown that they had come in search of his camp that night on the trail only to find he had escaped. Brown was told "there would have been some needed blood-letting" had he been caught. Troopers provided an armed escort for the Indiana wagons all the way from the Idaho Territory to the Sacramento Valley. In addition, the army delayed the Missouri party until the Indiana group was safely on its way.

The Brown family made their way to Red Bluff, where, in stark contrast to the Missouri reception, they were warmly greeted by the community. The *Red Bluff Independent* reported the arrival of a large emigrant train from the East: "Among the number were the wife, son, and three daughters of John Brown the hero of Harpers Ferry." The hero's son found work clearing fields of scrub oak and soon earned enough money to buy his own spread. Within a year, Brown had a sheep ranch of 128 acres and a reputation for producing some of the finest wool and Merino ewes in the region.

Like his father, Salmon Brown chose to live in a mixed-race community, and he hired hands of all races and backgrounds. In the spring of 1866, Brown hired a number of sheep shearers who were ex-Confederate soldiers. When it came time for the evening meal, one of Brown's regular hands, an African American named Scott, took his usual seat at the table. This was too much for the southerners, who declared "they did not mind working with a Negro, but they were not going to eat with him!" Scott left the table and returned a few moments later brandishing an axe and declaring, "If there is any man here who will not eat with a colored man just let him come forward!" No one came forward or said a word, and who sat at the supper table was never again an issue on Salmon Brown's ranch.

One night, Brown attended a big dance that attracted stockmen from all over Northern California. Brown recalled that there were white men and Spanish ladies, "Mexicans, half-breeds and Negros. It was a pretty mixed assembly, but they all ate, drank, and danced and spent the night in merriment." Brown could not help but notice a number of ex-Confederate soldiers there who were getting along harmoniously with everyone.

Brown inherited his father's talent for sheep farming. By 1890, he had built an empire of three thousand acres with fourteen thousand sheep, but

Salmon Brown praised living in Portland, which is shown in this 1903 photograph. *Oregon Historical Society #bb000227.*

the winter that was approaching would be legendary for its harshness. Heavy snow began falling in October; mud slides wiped out crops; locomotives were buried by avalanches in mountain passes and rescue teams were dispatched to dig out survivors. Brown lost three-fourths of his sheep, and it took everything he had left to pay his debts. Once again, a destitute Salmon Brown loaded his wagon and headed for a fresh start. This time he traveled up the Pacific coast and arrived in Salem in the summer of 1891. The Browns spent a few years in Salem rebuilding their fortunes before making a final move to Portland.

In 1902 and again in 1910, the great Oregon Trail pioneer Ezra Meeker made well-publicized journeys over the immigrant path he had traveled more than a half century before. Brown gave serious consideration to joining Meeker on the 1910 journey, retracing the path he himself had once traversed. In the end, Brown decided against the effort. He had traveled more of the country than almost anyone, and he was dead set against leaving Portland, of which he stated: "I have never seen a city so favorably situated to make a great city, nor have I seen another city where I would rather make my home."

LAST DAYS

Brown was in his late seventies when he was thrown from a horse. The fall shattered Brown's leg and hip and left him an invalid. No longer able to work his farm, Brown and his wife moved in with their daughter Agnes and her husband, George Evans, in a home located at 2024 East Couch Street in Portland. Evans, an Australian, made his living as an automobile mechanic.

Even fifty years after his father's death, Brown remained a celebrity who was sought out by admirers of his father and the occasional curious gawker. In 1914, the *Portland Journal* published a lengthy interview with Brown. Reporter Fred Lockley concluded his article by writing, "Salmon Brown is a gigantic chip off the old block in his appearance. His resemblance to John Brown's portrait is striking. A man of low voice and unassuming manners, he impresses as one of the genuine old fighting stock to which he belongs."

Brown lived with the Evanses about five years and was eighty-two when he ended his life. As John Brown's last surviving son, the news of Salmon Brown's demise made headlines. The *Portland Journal* wrote, "The last

Salmon Brown. *Courtesy of the Scott-Thomas Family Archives.*

chapter of the old border days, when strife was stirring for the break of the Civil War, came to a close yesterday with the funeral service for Salmon Brown…son of John Brown of Harpers Ferry, crusading abolitionist and sworn foe of slavery." Members of the Grand Army of the Republic served as pallbearers at Brown's funeral, and he was laid to rest with Civil War veterans in Portland's GAR Cemetery. Abbie Brown died in 1929 and is buried next to her husband. Their son, Dr. John Brown, a Portland dentist named for his famous grandfather, shares the family plot with his parents. Salmon Brown's inscription reads, "96th N.Y. Vol. Infantry. Son of John Brown of Kansas and Harpers Ferry renown."

Angels of the Battlefield

Oregon Women Who Served as Civil War Nurses

Like many dreamers before them, Mary and James Balmer left England for a better life in America. Mr. Balmer was a county tax collector in Shropshire but aspired to own his own land. In 1857, he kissed his wife and daughter goodbye and sailed from Liverpool to New York City. Taking whatever work he could find, it took him a year to scrape and save enough coin to purchase transatlantic passage for Mary and young Sarah. The Balmer ladies arrived in New York on October 20, 1858, aboard the SS *Lucy Thompson*. Reunited with James, the trio made their way to Prophetstown, a tiny hamlet on the rolling prairies of northern Illinois. The Balmer family earned their living farming, but just two years after settling down, their fresh start was turned upside down by the American Civil War.

When America beat the drum for volunteers to preserve the Union, James Balmer answered the call—and so did Mary! Balmer enlisted as a private in the 46th Illinois Volunteer Infantry. His regiment trained in Cairo, Illinois, and then was sent to the front lines in Tennessee. Not content to be the girl he left behind, Mary Balmer placed her daughter in the care of neighbors and made her way to the Federal army camp where the Illinois boys had been sent. At the Battle of Fort Donelson, both husband and wife would receive the baptism of war.

Fort Donelson, the Confederate bastion on the Cumberland River, was strategic to the Union advance in the West. The Federal forces were commanded by an obscure general named Ulysses S. Grant. Balmer's regiment was part of a brigade led by General Lew Wallace, who would become famous after the war for writing the novel *Ben Hur*. For five days, Grant pounded the Rebel fortifications with cannonballs from land and barrages from Union gunboats on the river. Wallace's brigade was in the center of the blue line on February 15, 1862, and they bore the brunt of a brutal Confederate assault as the Southerners attempted to break out of the siege. James Balmer was in the middle of the fight as the enemy was repelled with heavy casualties. The next day, Confederate general Simon Buckner sent Grant a message requesting terms of surrender. Grant responded, "No terms except unconditional and immediate surrender can be accepted." U.S. Grant became Unconditional Surrender Grant, and a legend was born.

It is said of the Civil War that when the fighting was over, the dying began. There had never been greater casualties in any conflict in American history, and neither side was prepared to deal with the carnage. Nursing and the care of wounded soldiers was considered the bloody work of men, but that tradition would transform out of necessity. It was in the aftermath of Fort Donelson that Mary Balmer met a true angel of the battlefield: Mother Bickerdyke.

Mary Ann Bickerdyke was a middle-aged widow from the same part of northern Illinois as the Balmers. She had followed the troops south with $500 in medical supplies donated by her hometown, and just as Mary Balmer had done, she volunteered as a nurse. Assigned to the field hospital at Fort Donelson, Bickerdyke was soon running the place. Known for her outspokenness and disregard for traditional military protocol, Bickerdyke was sometimes resented by senior officers but was called "mother" by the wounded boys she cared for. Later in the war, when an officer complained to William Tecumseh Sherman that Bickerdyke was ignoring established procedures, the general threw up his hands and exclaimed, "She outranks me. There is nothing I can do!"

Mary Balmer and the other nurses in Mother Bickerdyke's charge bathed and cleaned the wounded men, changed their bandages and kept the patients' hair cut short to prevent lice. They worked around the clock and suffered many a heartbreak as the angel of death visited the hospital. Balmer worked herself to the point of exhaustion, and her own health began to fail. Mother Bickerdyke sent her home to Illinois to rest and recover. On the front lines, Private Balmer learned that his wife had fallen ill and requested leave to tend to one who had cared for so many of his comrades. Leave was granted, but on the journey home, Balmer also fell ill.

As Balmer lay sick in a Union hospital near Memphis, word was sent to his wife that his condition was grave. Mary Balmer immediately started south. She would nurse her husband back to health as she had done with so many of the boys in blue. Alas, her journey was in vain. She arrived at the camp hospital to learn that the tax man from Shropshire had perished days before her arrival. Despite her tragedy, Mary Balmer once again volunteered as a nurse. She rejoined Mother Bickerdyke and was present at the fall of Vicksburg on July 4, 1863.

Widow Balmer was thirty-eight years old in the summer of 1863 when she fell in love with a soldier fourteen years her junior. Jacob Hartman was a German-born veteran of the Battle of Shiloh who served as a private in the 18th Missouri Regiment. The couple was married on August 9, 1863, and the new husband insisted that Mary remove herself from the danger of the battlefield. Mary agreed, but she could not abandon her boys, so she took a nursing position at Jefferson General Hospital in Indiana. While Mary toiled in the hospital, Jacob Hartman and his regiment marched to the sea with Sherman.

Jefferson Hospital was the third-largest military facility in the Civil War. It consisted of twenty-seven long buildings arranged in a circular pattern like the spokes of a wheel. Each of the buildings held fifty-three beds for patients and one bed for the ward master. Operating the last two years of the war, Jefferson Hospital treated over sixteen thousand wounded soldiers. Mary Balmer Hartman worked at this hospital and two others until the war ended and her soldier came marching home.

The safest place for a soldier in the Civil War may have been on the battlefield. Of the 600,000 deaths in the war, two-thirds of the fatalities were not from battle wounds but were due to disease. Dysentery, tuberculosis, pneumonia and measles claimed more victims than the cannonball or bayonet. There was little scientific knowledge of germs or how infection was spread. Army camps were established based on strategic necessity and not purposeful planning. Latrines overflowed into drinking water. Horses and men swam and drank from the same creeks. Troops slept literally in piles of men for warmth. Surgeons didn't even wash their hands, let alone their instruments, as they moved from patient to patient. The most common surgical procedure was amputation. It was in these conditions that brave and patriotic women volunteered to work.

In Washington, D.C., Dorothea Dix organized a formal nursing corps. Dix wanted to ensure that the nursing ranks were not infiltrated by young marriage-minded women. She required that her nurses be plain looking and middle aged and required them to wear black or gray dresses with no bows or ruffles. Her nurses nicknamed her "Dragon Dix," but as many as two thousand women formally served in established hospitals of the U.S. Medical Department. Thousands of others, like Mary Balmer Hartman, served as volunteers on the

Civil War nurse Clara Barton went on to found the American Red Cross. *Library of Congress.*

battlefields. One of those volunteers was a clerk at the U.S. Patent Office named Clara Barton. Determined to do her part for the war effort, Barton worked in hospitals and the front lines and raised thousands of dollars for medical supplies while never accepting a salary for herself. After the war, she continued her mercy work and founded the American Red Cross.

When the war ended, Mary Balmer Hartman joined her husband in Missouri. Hartman made his living as a cooper, a maker of barrels, and eventually brought his trade to Oregon. Unlike many nurses whose work went unrecognized and unrewarded, Mary qualified for and received an old age veteran's pension of twelve dollars per month The couple lived in a house on Eleventh Street in Portland, and when Mary died in 1905 at the age of eighty, the *Oregonian* printed her obituary under the headline "Civil War Veteran Dies." She was laid to rest in the GAR Cemetery among the veterans she had cared for forty years earlier. Jacob Hartman died nine years later and is buried next to his wife. At least two other Civil War nurses are buried in the GAR Cemetery: Elizabeth Jane Beamer and Rose Atkinson. Jennie Beamer and her veteran husband moved to Oregon after the war. She went on to serve as state chaplain of the Women's Relief Corps, which assisted soldiers and veterans much as today's USO does. Rose Atkinson, who served as an army nurse and hospital matron, became senior vice-president of the Oregon WRC.

NURSES REST IN EUGENE

Two other Civil War nurses rest in Eugene Pioneer Cemetery, 110 miles south of Portland. A few days before she was to be married, Thirsa Burris's fiancé enlisted in the Union army. The wedding took place as planned, but just days later, bridegroom Warden Willis Gossett and three of Thirsa's brothers marched off to war with the 77th Ohio Infantry. Thirsa Gossett volunteered for the medical corps and was assigned to a hospital in Evansville, Indiana. For two years, she tended to sick and wounded soldiers, changing their dressings and washing their clothes. One of her patients may have been her own husband, who was wounded at the Battle of Shiloh. Ward Gossett, whom Thirsa called "my dear soldier boy," was injured badly enough that he was discharged from the army in 1862. Despite his war wounds and Thirsa's demanding hospital schedule, their first child, daughter Hortensia, was born in July 1863. Motherhood ended Thirsa's nursing career.

In the 1880s, Ward and Thirsa Gossett and their two daughters left their Ohio farm. Along with the family of Thirsa's sister, who was also married to a Union veteran, they moved to Oregon. They lived in Eugene, Springfield and Junction City. The men were active members of the GAR, and Thirsa and her sister Melissa Burris Brabham were active in the Ladies of the GAR. Thirsa died in 1913 at the age of sixty-one. The Eugene tent of the Daughters of Union Veterans of the Civil War is named in her honor.

Thirsa and Ward Gossett. When her husband and brothers marched off to war, Thirsa Gossett volunteered as a Union army nurse. *Courtesy of William Reid.*

Not far from the graves of the Gossetts stands a marble tower marking the final resting place of another angel of the battlefield: Elizabeth McNett Rehm. Elizabeth was single and thirty years old when the Civil War began, an old maid by the standards of her day. A native of New York, we know little about her Civil War service except that she served in the U.S. Medical Corps and qualified for a veteran's pension. After the war, Elizabeth McNett married William Rehm, who was eighteen years younger than her, and the couple had one child, a daughter, Maria. The Rehms headed west to Oregon

The Army and Navy Nurses Memorial at Arlington National Cemetery. *Library of Congress.*

and claimed a farm in Umatilla County. Around the turn of the century, tragedy struck as Rehm's husband and daughter died. She moved to Eugene.

William Rehm left Elizabeth well off financially, and she became an early benefactor of Eugene Bible University, today's Northwest Christian University. When Mrs. Rehm died in 1915 at the advanced age of eighty-four, the *Eugene Guard* ran a lengthy obituary that stated that she had died in Rehm Hall, a university building named in her honor and where she had lived for the past seven or eight years. There was no mention of her participation in the Civil War. Mrs. Rehm is buried beneath a towering Douglas fir, and an elegant white marble obelisk marks her grave. Although we know little about her Civil War contributions, we do know that she was immensely proud of her service. The epitaph carved on her stone monument reads succinctly "Civil War Nurse."

Historical records for the nursing corps are minimal; therefore, the women who volunteered are largely anonymous. Somewhere between two and eight thousand women served as nurses for the Union army. The number on the Confederate side is believed to be significantly lower due to traditional cultural differences between North and South. An examination of available records indicates that at least fifteen Union nurses made their way to Oregon after the Civil War and ended their days there.

NAME	CEMETERY
Rose Martin Atkinson	GAR Cemetery, Portland
Martha Bamford	Rest Lawn, Junction City
Elizabeth Jane Beamer	GAR Cemetery, Portland
Jennie Evans Epperly	Unknown, lived in Portland 1893
Thirsa Gossett	Eugene Pioneer Cemetery
Mary Balmer Hartman	GAR Cemetery, Portland
Mildred Conklin Hilton	Unknown, died Portland 1927
Etta Hubbs	Lebanon IOOF Cemetery
Ann Lester	Creswell Cemetery, unmarked
Louisa Nichols McDowell	Dallas Cemetery
Charlotte Olney	Lone Fir Cemetery, Portland—unmarked
Elizabeth Rehm	Eugene Pioneer Cemetery
Elizabeth Smaldren	Lone Fir Cemetery, Portland
Mandana C. Thorp	Unknown, died Portland 1916
Elizabeth Wood	Douglass Cemetery, Troutdale

The Last Oregon Confederate

He Rode with Cole Younger and Frank James

Frank Hunter was just sixty days short of his 100th birthday when he drew his last breath. With Hunter's passing, another chapter in Oregon's hidden history of the Civil War came to a close. The old man, who had ridden with Frank James and Cole Younger, was Oregon's last surviving Confederate veteran.

Francis Marion Hunter was born in Missouri on January 21, 1846. His parents, William and Maria Hunter, who had come to Missouri from North Carolina, named Frank after a Revolutionary War hero. The family lived far from the border wars with Kansas, and when Fort Sumter was fired on, the Civil War seemed like a faraway event. Hunter was sixteen in the summer of 1862, when the Civil War arrived in his hometown of Lone Jack.

The town took its name from an old, gnarled and knotty black jack tree that stood on the apex of a little prairie knoll. Word was received that a column of Union cavalry, 750 men strong, was riding on Lone Jack. The Federals were out to retaliate against Confederate forces in the area for a defeat they had suffered at the hands of William Quantrill a few days earlier. The call went out for volunteers, and Frank, along with brothers Robert and Archie, joined Captain Upton Hays in the Jackson County Cavalry. The Hunter boys had been in the army just two days when the shooting started. Union troopers opened fire at sunrise with fusillades from a battery of Indiana artillery. The Federal troops were well supplied with horses, equipment, ammunition and uniforms. The Missouri Confederates were an irregular force with little in the way of proper military attire. They were armed with shotguns and

Frank and Mary Hunter had this portrait made in Hood River. *Courtesy of Shannon Carroll LeHuquet.*

squirrel rifles and had little ammunition, but they were on their home turf, and they fought like wildcats.

Hays's cavalry fought dismounted, and they charged the Union cannon, seizing the big guns in a fierce fight. The blue cavalry mounted a counterattack that sent Hunter and his comrades scurrying for cover behind a fence. As the defending forces ran low on ammunition, a lone rider appeared, dashing up and down the Confederate lines, tossing soldiers packs of ammo that he carried in his hat. The fearless rider was Cole Younger, and his courage was nothing short of breathtaking. He galloped his horse full tilt in plain view of enemy troops just 150 yards away. Every man in blue aimed to bring Younger down, but every bullet missed its mark, although Younger did write years later that several rounds had passed through his clothing.

The battle raged back and forth for more than five hours. With fresh ammunition, the Jackson County men made another charge against the artillery and again killed or drove back the defenders. This time, the Indiana cannons stayed in Rebel hands, and the men from Lone Jack would use them throughout the remainder of the war. With the artillery in the hands of the Rebels, the Federal troops fell back into the town, where the battle turned into a hand-to-hand street fight. Kit Dalton, a Confederate soldier at Lone Jack, described the scene in the town: "Pistols, gun stocks, rocks, planks from the sidewalks, pickets jeered from fences were in common use in this fierce struggle, and brute strength played no inconsiderable part in the slaughter."

The Union men retreated to the town's hotel, and from this sheltered position, they poured murderous volley fire from the second story into Lone

Jack's defenders. Trapped and outnumbered, the invading Federals refused to surrender because they feared the enemy they were facing was William Quantrill's men. Quantrill was a guerrilla leader with a merciless reputation for murdering prisoners, but he was not at this battle. Because the trapped men would not surrender, the order was given to set fire to the hotel.

Younger volunteered to set the incendiaries and was joined on the mission by ten men, including Frank James. After the war, the Younger brothers, along with Frank and Jesse James, would become the world-famous outlaws who gave the Wild West its nickname. However, on this day, Younger and James were just teenagers like Frank Hunter and in a fight for their lives. The eleven volunteers sprinted through a hail of bullets to throw flaming turpentine balls through the first-floor hotel windows. Of the eleven who rushed the hotel, only two in addition to Younger and James made it back alive.

The Union men held out until the flaming building started to collapse around them, sending many men to a fiery grave. Finally, the soldiers fled into the street, where they surrendered only after another fierce round of hand-to-hand combat. Contrary to their expectations, the prisoners were well treated and given parole after agreeing not to fight again. Only the wounded Federal commander was singled out for mistreatment, and that was quickly put to a halt by Younger.

Frank Hunter and his brothers had successfully defended their hometown in the Battle of Lone Jack. They would serve for another two and a half years, all the way to the end of the war. Following the victory at Lone Jack, Upton Hays was promoted to colonel, and the Confederate forces withdrew to Arkansas, where they continued to operate as an irregular unit under Quantrill. In September 1862, Hays attacked a Union force at Newtonia, Missouri. Although the battle resulted in another Confederate triumph, Hays was killed by a bullet to the head.

Following Colonel Hays's death, the Jackson County Cavalry was reorganized into the regular Confederate army as the 12th Missouri Cavalry Regiment. Frank Hunter served under General Sterling Price and fought valiantly at the Battle of Mark's Mills. Outgunned and outmanned, Confederate armies were defeated. Robert E. Lee surrendered in Virginia, but Sterling Price refused to surrender in the West. He took the men who would follow him and fled into Mexico. The motion picture *The Undefeated*, starring John Wayne and Rock Hudson, is based on Price's Mexican adventure.

Frank Hunter was more pragmatic than his general. Nineteen when the war ended, Hunter chose Missouri over Mexico. He hoped to begin a peaceful life, but at home, radicals pushed through a new state constitution

PVT
FRANCIS M HUNTER
CO G 12 MO CAV
CSA
JAN 21 1846
NOV 16 1945

Tradition holds that Confederate headstones are pointed on top to keep Yankees from sitting on them. *Photo by Penny Kennedy.*

that barred Confederate sympathizers from voting, serving on juries, holding public office, preaching the gospel or carrying out any number of public roles. The Younger and James brothers opted for an outlaw life, while the Hunter brothers chose to go west. Frank married Mary Evelinah Evans, and they started a farm in Kansas, where daughter Hattie and son Price were born.

Eventually, the Hunter family settled in Mosier, a tiny hamlet located on the cliffs of the Columbia River in Wasco County. Mosier is eight miles east of Hood River and even today has a population of fewer than five hundred. Frank and his brother Bob were partners in a dairy farm and a cherry orchard. Bob passed away in 1895, but Frank lived another fifty years. When Frank died on November 16, 1945, he was mourned by his son and daughter, nineteen grandchildren and eighteen great-grandchildren.

When Union Civil War veterans immigrated to Oregon, they established seventy-six chapters of their fraternal organization, the Grand Army of the Republic. There were GAR posts in every corner of the state, and when a Union veteran died, he received an elaborate military funeral and was often buried under a government-issued headstone identifying him as a Civil War soldier. There is written documentation of ten thousand Union veterans who lived in Oregon, but not so with the Confederate veterans. Frank Hunter must have been one of thousands of ex-Confederates, especially from the border states like Missouri, who came to Oregon. Yet the Sons of Confederate Veterans have documented fewer than two hundred Oregon grave sites of Confederate vets. Oregon had no chapters of the United Confederate Veterans; there were no conventions to attend and no formal records kept. Frank Hunter's grave is one of the few that has an official Confederate military headstone. He is buried in Mosier Cemetery.

Oregon's Last Union Veterans

One Was Famous, the Other Was Not

Theodore Penland did more for the Union army after the Civil War was over than he ever did as a teenage soldier in the 152nd Indiana Volunteer Infantry. When Penland celebrated his 101st birthday in Portland, he was one of a handful of living Civil War veterans and was the last commander in chief of the Grand Army of the Republic.

Penland was born in New Paris, Indiana, and was just twelve years old when Fort Sumter was fired upon. He watched as his father and older brothers enlisted in the Union army and marched off to war. Penland's father, John, was killed in action at Stone's River. Two of the bothers were captured and sent to the notorious Andersonville prison camp. Enlistment age in the Union army was eighteen, and young Theodore was twice turned away by recruiters when he tried to sign up. The tenacious farm boy would not give up, but he had been raised to believe that it was a sin to lie, so he devised an ingenious scheme to fight for his county. Taking two slips of paper, Penland wrote the number "18" on each of them and put them in his boots. When the recruiting sergeant asked the recruit if he was eighteen or over, sixteen-year-old Penland snapped, "I am over eighteen now!"

Private Penland's regiment was dispatched to West Virginia. The 152nd did not fight any battles but guarded the strategic river crossing at Harpers Ferry. Penland served six months at the end of the war and mustered out of the army on August 30, 1865. Penland returned to the farm in Indiana, but when he finally turned eighteen, the lure of adventure propelled him west. Bound for California, Penland only had enough money for train fare to Wyoming, so he walked the last thousand miles from Cheyenne to Sacramento.

In California, Penland found work with the Union Pacific Railroad and built tracks through the Sierra Nevada Mountains. He stayed with Union Pacific until the golden spike was driven at Promontory Point, after which he returned to the Indiana farm, but the call of the West was too strong to resist. Penland stayed on the move, first to Michigan and then west to Los Angeles and San Diego. He worked as a butcher and a teamster and was in his seventies when he moved to Portland to manage a boardinghouse on Front Street.

Penland, like hundreds of thousands of Union veterans, joined the GAR. The Union veterans' group lobbied for pension benefits and put its stamp on the written history of the Civil War. The GAR founded our modern Memorial Day and promoted the flying of the U.S. flag at every schoolhouse in America. GAR monuments were erected in front of courthouses and cemeteries everywhere. Six of the seven U.S. presidents after Lincoln were Civil War veterans. Starting in 1866, the GAR held annual conventions, called encampments. Penland was at the very first GAR encampment in

The year 1939 was the last one that Civil War veterans marched in Salem's Memorial Day Parade. George Kingsbury, ninety-five (center left), was commander of the Idaho GAR. Thomas Jackson, ninety-seven (center right), was from Mill City. *Salem Public Library Historic Photograph Collection.*

Indianapolis and at the last encampment held in that same city in 1949. In the eighty-three years in between, he missed just two of the annual meetings. Penland steadily advanced in the ranks of the GAR; in Portland, he was commander of the Sumner post and became head of the Department of Oregon. On the national level, Penland served as patriotic instructor and was elected junior and senior vice-commander.

The work of the GAR became Penland's full-time avocation. He enjoyed giving talks on his experiences in the war, of the time he saw President Lincoln and on the virtues of living carefully. He favored talking and singing on the radio; his distinctive singing voice was a feature of GAR firesides, with his favorite song reportedly "Tenting on the Old Camp Ground." Penland appeared in *LIFE* magazine four times, appeared on the Ralph Edwards radio program *This Is Your Life* and was featured in over 350 articles published in national and international newspapers. He visited Australia and New Zealand and also spoke at the launching of two U.S. Navy battleships during World War II.

In the 1890s, GAR encampments would host twenty-five thousand attendees, but by the 1948 encampment, fewer than a dozen Civil War veterans were healthy enough to attend. It was decided that 1949 would

Civil War veterans George H. Jones of Maine (left) and Theodore A. Penland of Oregon confer at the 1945 National Encampment of the GAR. *Courtesy of Richard Penland.*

be the final encampment. At that final muster, the six Union veterans in attendance elected Theodore Augustus Penland as their commander in chief. They also decided that there would be no further elections, which made Penland the last commander of the GAR.

Penland outlived two wives and fathered eleven children. In September 1950, the 101-year-old GAR commander flew from Portland to Los Angeles for a speaking engagement. Upon his return to Portland a week later, he felt tired and checked into the veterans' hospital in Vancouver. Penland answered his final roll call on September

13, 1950. At the time of his death, Penland held membership in thirty-two patriotic orders, including the GAR. He was laid to rest in Portland Memorial Mausoleum.

WHO WAS OREGON'S LAST CIVIL WAR VETERAN?

Theodore Penland was widely acclaimed as the last Civil War veteran in Oregon, and upon his death, the Oregon GAR ceased to exist. Newspapers around the world noted his passing, but eighty miles south of Portland, in the Linn County timber town of Lebanon, was another claimant to the title of last Civil War veteran. James W. Smith was 108 years old when Penland died. Smith served in an obscure forty-man cavalry unit that patrolled the Columbia Gorge. The unit was officially designated Olney's

Sons of Union Veterans of the Civil War members in Lebanon dedicate the grave of James W. Smith, Oregon's last Civil War veteran. *Courtesy of Ken Jacobsen.*

Detachment of Oregon Cavalry, and it served from July 12 to October 31, 1864. Led by brothers Nathan and Orville Olney, the detachment was meant to supplement the 1st Oregon Cavalry Regiment, but it was poorly trained, undisciplined and had a reputation for misappropriating and selling government property, as well as "fundraising" from the citizens it was sworn to protect. The regular soldiers with whom these men served called them "Olney's Forty Thieves." The unit was disbanded after ninety days, and thus ended Smith's military career.

Smith died on March 22, 1951. He never saw any action or came within one thousand miles of a Confederate soldier. He lived a quiet life and never joined the GAR or applied for a Civil War pension. Yet Smith outlived Penland by six months. In 2010, the Sons of Union Veterans of the Civil War affixed a brass plaque to Smith's headstone in Lebanon's IOOF Cemetery, officially declaring him the last Civil War veteran in Oregon. A special graveside ceremony was held, complete with a musket salute and taps.

The last surviving veteran of the American Civil War was Penland's friend and GAR colleague Albert Woolson of Minnesota. Woolson died in 1956 at the age of 109.

Appendix

A Few Good Men

More Noteworthy Oregon Civil War Veterans

All veterans deserve to be remembered, but space limits the number of Oregonians whose history can be documented in this book. Listed here are a few more soldiers whose achievements reflect well on the two million Americans who served in the Civil War.

Joseph Eaton is one of two Civil War generals buried in Oregon. *Library of Congress.*

JOSEPH EATON, along with Thomas Thorp, is one of just two Civil War generals buried in Oregon. A native of New York, Eaton graduated from West Point in the class of 1835, which included George Meade. Twice cited for gallantry in the Mexican War, Eaton served as an aide to general and future president Zachary Taylor. An outstanding staff officer, Eaton was assigned as the army's assistant paymaster during the Civil War, rising to the rank of brevet brigadier general. After the war, Eaton was appointed chief paymaster of the Department of the Pacific. He was stationed at Fort Vancouver but chose to make his home in Portland, where he was an avid fly fisherman. Eaton retired from the army after fifty years of service. His obituary in the *Oregonian* noted, "Nothing afforded him more genuine pleasure than an excursion to one of the local trout streams." As a young officer posted to the New Mexico frontier, Eaton sketched a series of watercolors that are among the earliest recorded images of the region. It is for these paintings that Eaton is best remembered today. His work is featured in the prestigious Zaplin Lambert Gallery in Santa Fe. General Eaton is buried in Portland's Riverside Cemetery.

RODOLPH CRANDALL was a two-time mayor of Hillsboro and also served as Washington County's treasurer and assessor before being elected to the bench. In 1881, Crandall was one of the founding members of the Hillsboro Fire Department. During the Civil War, Crandall was a captain in the 5th Iowa Cavalry and fought under Grant at Fort Donelson and under George Thomas at Nashville. Judge Crandall was post commander of the GAR. He is buried in Hillsboro Pioneer Cemetery.

MEDOREM CRAWFORD was an Oregon pioneer who arrived with the Elijah White wagon train in 1842. A year later, he voted for the formation of the provisional government at Champoeg. In 1844, his son was the first white child born west of the Willamette River. Crawford served in the provisional and territorial legislatures and, after statehood, was elected from Yamhill County to the Oregon House of Representatives, where he supported the election of Edward D. Baker to the U.S. Senate. Crawford was visiting his father in New York when the Civil War began. Volunteering his services, he was commissioned by President Lincoln as captain of U.S. Volunteers and charged with escorting wagon trains over the Oregon Trail. He recruited a one-hundred-man cavalry company and personally made the cross-country trek at least twice. After the war, Crawford was appointed by President Grant to a number of federal offices in Oregon. Crawford also served as president of the Oregon Pioneer Association. Captain Crawford retired to his farm in Dayton and is buried in Brookside Cemetery. His son, Medorem Crawford Jr., was one of the first Oregonians appointed to West Point and retired from the army as a one-star general. General Crawford is buried in Arlington National Cemetery.

WILLIAM PAINE LORD was the ninth governor of Oregon. An attorney, Lord served as a major in the 1st Delaware Cavalry. He fought in a famous battle near Westminster, Maryland, where a mounted charge delayed Fitzhugh Lee's Confederate cavalry on its way to Gettysburg. Lord remained in the army

William Lord is the only Oregon governor who was a Civil War veteran. *Courtesy of Oregon State Library.*

after the Civil War and was dispatched to Alaska to oversee its transfer from Russia to the United States. In 1870, Lord established a law practice in Salem and was elected to the state senate and then to the Oregon Supreme Court. A Republican, Justice Lord was elected governor in 1894. He served one term before being appointed minister to Argentina by President McKinley. Lord retired to San Francisco in 1910, but when he died, his body was returned to Salem, where it is interred in Mount Crest Abbey Mausoleum.

WALLACE BALDWIN came to Oregon after the Civil War via ship to Panama, crossing the isthmus and then boarding another ship to Portland. Wallace had served in the 103rd Ohio Infantry but was discharged due to disability. Once recovered, he reenlisted in the 150th Ohio and fought in the repulse of Jubal Early's raid on Washington. In Oregon, Baldwin was appointed postmaster of Corvallis and then served as Benton County treasurer and one term as mayor of Corvallis. He married Adelaide Brownson of Philomath and was a partner in Woodcock & Baldwin hardware business. Governor Zenas Moody appointed Baldwin state fish commissioner. Mayor Baldwin is buried in Corvallis's Crystal Lake Cemetery.

FRANCIS M. JACKSON settled in Oregon in 1859 but returned to his home in Tennessee when the Civil War began. Jackson served as a captain in the 4th Tennessee Cavalry until he was wounded at Chattanooga and spent eighteen months as a prisoner of war. After the war, Jackson returned to Oregon and settled in the Hood River Valley, where he served as director of the Pine Grove schools. The ex-Confederate officer was warmly welcomed at local GAR meetings. Captain Jackson is buried in a family cemetery on his old homestead south of Hood River.

JAMES M. LEWELLING lived in Newberg for forty years, but few people knew he was a Civil War veteran. He rarely spoke of his experience with the 22nd Indiana Infantry and gave almost all of his pension check to the American Bible Institute. When Lewelling died in 1935, found among his effects was a letter from President Franklin Roosevelt recognizing him as the last surviving member of the honor guard stationed by the body of President Lincoln as it lay in the Indiana statehouse before burial. Lewelling rests in the Friends Cemetery in Newberg.

THOMAS C. WYMAN enlisted in the Union army the day of the First Battle of Bull Run. As a private in the 2nd Maine Volunteer Infantry, he fought in Second Bull Run, Antietam, Fredericksburg and Chancellorsville. When the 2nd Maine completed two years of service on May 20, 1863, Wyman, who had signed up for three years, was transferred to the 20th Maine. Two weeks later, he took part in the famous bayonet charge down Little Round Top. Despite being shot in the left leg, Wyman completed his service and mustered out of the army in October 1864. He returned home to Maine, but when his brother was drafted into the navy, Wyman took his place as a substitute and served as a landsman

on the sailing frigate USS *Sabine*. After the war, Wyman came to Oregon, where he served as the lighthouse keeper at the Cape Arago lighthouse in Coos Bay. In those days, the only access to the lighthouse was by a hand-cranked cable tramway. In 1898, disaster struck as the four-hundred-foot-long cable snapped, sending Wyman, his daughter and two other individuals plunging to the rocky surf sixty feet below. All parties survived, but Wyman lost his leg. Just a month later, a bridge to the lighthouse was completed. Wyman is buried in Marshfield Pioneer Cemetery.

Cape Arago lighthouse keeper Thomas Wyman, shown here in 1897, fought on Little Round Top with the 20th Maine. *Courtesy of Coos Historical & Maritime Museum.*

Bibliography

Manuscripts

"Alaric B. Chapin Archives." Glenbow Museum, Calgary, Alberta.
Edgerton, Edward G.C. "Nathan Huntley Edgerton," 1932. Courtesy of Nancy Anders and Colonel Daniel Edgerton.
Fleming, Kenneth M. "Thomas Clinton Lovett Hatcher 1839–1861," 2011.
McArthur, Scott "The Life of a Soldier," 2008.
Oregon DUVCW. "Thirsa Gossett," 2008.

Newspapers

Corvallis Gazette Times
Eugene Register Guard
Hood River News
Oneonta [New York] *Star*
Oregonian
Portland Journal

Books

Beyer, W.F., and O.F. Keydel, eds. *Deeds of Valor*. Detroit, MI: Perrien-Keydel Company, 1907.
Jones, J.W. *The Story of American Heroism*. Springfield, OH: Werner Company, 1897.

McPherson, James, and Patricia McPherson, eds. *Lamson of the Gettysburg: The Civil War Letters of Lieutenant Roswell H. Lamson, U.S. Navy.* New York: Oxford University Press, 1997.

Swanson, James L. *Manhunt: The 12-Day Chase for Lincoln's Killer.* New York: HarperCollins, 2006.

ARTICLES

Bennett, Tom, and George Edmonston Jr. "The Presidency of Benjamin Lee Arnold." *OSU Alumni Association*, 2000.

Edmonston, George. "In Memory of Bell Field" and "They Were Soldiers Once." *OSU Alumni Association*, 2004.

Lockwood, H.C. "The Capture of Fort Fisher." *Atlantic Monthly*, June 1871.

McArthur, Scott. "Military Justice: Law and Order, Oregon and the Civil War." *Oregon State Bar Bulletin*, August 2004.

Stanford, Phil. "Smile When You Say That, Pardner." *Oregonian*, September 2, 1991.

Weber, Sandra. "John Brown's Family: A Living Legacy." *Civil War Times*, June 2006.

OFFICIAL RECORDS

Aney, Col. Warren W. "Records of the Oregon State Defense Force and Oregon National Guard," 2008–2011.

Doherty, Lt. Edward, "Capture of J. Wilkes Booth and David E. Herold." Official Report of the 16th NY Cavalry. April 26, 1865.

Merritt, Gen. Wesley. "Cedar Creek After Action Report." 1st Cavalry Division, USA. October 24, 1864.

Secretary of the Navy. *Official Records of the Union and Confederate Navies in the War of the Rebellion.* Washington, D.C.: Government Printing Office, 1900.

About the Author

R andol B. Fletcher, a lifelong student of history, is a fifth-generation Oregonian born and raised in Albany. He graduated from the University of Oregon with degrees in history and political science. Fletcher has been Civil War reenacting since 2003 and is often joined on his adventures by his wife, Karen, and their children, Andrew and Allison. As a member, and past camp commander, of the Sons of Union Veterans of the Civil War, Fletcher began researching the lives of Oregon Civil War soldiers while leading cemetery restoration projects in Eugene, Corvallis and Portland. His research led him to write a series of Civil War–themed articles for *Oregon Magazine*. Other publications where Fletcher's work has appeared include *Columbia Magazine* and *The Banner*.